INSPIRING DEEP LEARNING

WITH METACOGNITION

T0368855

INSPIRING DEEP LEARNING

WITH METACOGNITION

NATHAN BURNS

A Guide for Secondary Teaching

CORWIN

A SAGE Publishing Company

SAGE Publications Ltd
1 Oliver's Yard
55 City Road
London EC1Y 1SP

Corwin
A SAGE company
2455 Teller Road
Thousand Oaks, California 91320
(800)233-9936
www.corwin.com

SAGE Publications India Pvt Ltd
B 1/I 1 Mohan Cooperative Industrial Area
Mathura Road
New Delhi 110 044

SAGE Publications Asia-Pacific Pte Ltd
3 Church Street
#10-04 Samsung Hub
Singapore 049483

Editor: James Clark
Assistant editor: Diana Alves
Production editor: Martin Fox
Copyeditor: Neil Dowden
Proofreader: Derek Markham
Indexer: Judith Lavender
Marketing manager: Dilhara Attygalle
Cover design: Wendy Scott
Typeset by: C&M Digitals (P) Ltd, Chennai, India
Printed in the UK

Library of Congress Control Number: 2022945763

British Library Cataloguing in Publication data

A catalogue record for this book is available from the British Library

ISBN 978-1-5297-8972-0
ISBN 978-1-5297-8971-3 (pbk)

At SAGE we take sustainability seriously. Most of our products are printed in the UK using responsibly sourced papers and boards. When we print overseas we ensure sustainable papers are used as measured by the PREPS grading system. We undertake an annual audit to monitor our sustainability.

Contents

About the Author

Nathan Burns is currently the Head of Maths in a Derbyshire school. He has previously worked as an Assistant Progress and Achievement Leader for Key Stage 3, More Able and Talented Co-ordinator and as a Second in Maths. Aside from these roles, Nathan is a metacognitive researcher, dedicating his teaching career to researching and understanding the theory and its applications to the classroom.

Introduction

Learning Objectives

In this chapter we will:

- Understand the purpose of this book, and why it is worth you giving up the time to read it
- Outline the structure of the book and each chapter so there are no hidden surprises

Introduction

I really love metacognition. I guess if I did not, then I would not be writing this book. I genuinely believe that metacognition is an untapped area for teachers to explore. For some, you will have known about it since the 1980s, and perhaps believe that it is just one of those educational fads that is coming back into fashion again, but does not really work. I believe that the reason it has not worked is because it has not been done correctly. Why this is, I am not sure. Perhaps it is due to the slightly greater complexity of this theory than others that we try to implement within teaching. Perhaps it is because metacognitive teaching is only a subtle change-up from the high-quality teaching that you will be doing every single day, anyway. Whatever the reason, I still believe in the positive impact that metacognition can have on teachers and on student outcomes. I passionately believe that the strategies in this book will improve your teaching, and certainly improve the outcomes of the students that we work with.

Though this book may be targeted at secondary teachers – both newly qualified and experienced – there are strategies in this book that would work for students in any age group. Yes, they will need tweaking, but there are ideas in here to suit the early-years specialist right through to those leading adult education. As you will find out later in this book, metacognition is a constantly developing thing, right down from a wee youngster through to those in our old age. We are all metacognitive, at pretty much all stages in our life, and so it is reasonable that we always have the opportunity to improve this area of thinking.

The purpose of this book is to provide you with as many strategies as possible for your classroom. You may find the book seems a little light on theory, but this is purposeful. I could have written two hundred pages on the history and development of metacognition, but when it can be summarised in a couple of thousand words, this seems appropriate. There are further readings provided at the end of each chapter, as well a full bibliography at the end of the book if you do want to delve further. However, teachers are busy creatures, and finding the time to read this one book is difficult enough, let alone finding the time to read all of these additional papers and books that I have. So if you have the time, and the interest, go for it. But if not, do not despair, as years of courses, reading and research will be crammed into these pages for you.

How the Book Is Structured

You will also hopefully find that this book is extremely user friendly. Each chapter follows the same structure, as shown below:

- Learning objectives: A couple of bullet points summarising the key points being covered in that chapter.
- Introduction: A slightly more in-depth introduction to the ideas that are being introduced within that chapter.
- Summary: A few key bullet points from the chapter, so that you have got a quick reminder of everything that you have just read, as well as a quick point to flick back to as a reminder (rather than having to read through the chapter once again in full).
- Further reading: A brief list of texts that you may want to consider reading. Some or all of these may even be repeated in the references list at the end of the book.

As mentioned, the purpose of this book is to provide you with strategies that you can take away instantly and apply to your classroom. For this very reason, every single strategy within this book is laid out in exactly the same way, as follows:

- **What:** A very brief overview of what the strategy is, including any physical resources that you may need.
- **When/How:** A paragraph on when you could be using the strategies, and some top tips on how to use it effectively.
- **Why:** A link back to the theory, understanding the type of metacognitive thinking that the strategy mentioned will be seeking to improve.
- **Examples:** An example, either written by myself, or some of the excellent guest contributors, explaining when they use this strategy, and some further top tips and ideas.
- **Summary:** A further few bullet points summarising the strategy, again, as a final reminder and point of revision.

Fingers crossed this layout is well thought-out and helpful. You will also find that in other chapters there are infrequent but hugely helpful additional guest contributions. Again, these will help to shine a light on where this theory has been taken and applied so successfully into classrooms, giving you some great ideas yourself.

And last but not least there are also resources. Many of the resources mentioned within this book are already created, and available for free from a shared Google Drive folder, which can be accessed from my Twitter page @MrMetacognition. And if they are not already made, or if you have questions, comments or ideas, then you can get in touch: mrmetacognition@gmail.com

Summary

- The purpose of this book is to explore why metacognition is so powerful, and to give you a vast range of strategies that you can implement into your classroom, with little or no additional work, right now.
- Each chapter will follow the same layout, which has been designed for maximum user-friendliness.
- Resources mentioned within the book are already available, and where you have questions, comments, ideas or difficulties, you can get in touch with me directly.

1
Metacognitive Theory

Learning Objectives

In this chapter we will:

- Understand what metacognition is not
- Understand what metacognition *actually* is
- Explore the literature which shows the positive impact of metacognitive teaching
- Review reports from significant education bodies, such as the Education Endowment Foundation and the Office for Standards in Education.

Introduction

Metacognition is a historic theory, rather than a newly developed or refined pedagogy of the twenty-first century. Ideas around metacognition can be traced back to at least the early twentieth century, but were initially collected together by the superb academic Brown and DeLoache in 1978. This brilliant work was carried further by other important theorists, including Schraw (1998) and Flavell (2002). Therefore, it would be of no surprise if you have heard of metacognition before, seeing as it has been around in the (relative) mainstream of educational theory for close to half a century. For those involved in education over the previous two decades, you may have even been exposed to metacognitive changes in schools previously, perhaps under the guise of learning to learn. The aim of this chapter will be to develop a clear understanding of the nuts and bolts of metacognitive theory to ensure successful application of the strategies that come later in this book, but without overloading you or turning this into a difficult-to-digest and theory-heavy chapter! The chapter will begin with understanding what metacognition is *not*, before exploring potential definitions of metacognition, how the theory works and, finally, considering why metacognition is so important and worth your (and your school's) time and energy to implement.

What Metacognition Is Not

Before understanding what metacognition *is*, I really believe in the importance of understanding what it is *not*. Often, metacognition and self-regulation are seen as synonyms.

However, this is incorrect. Self-regulation is a greater idea, or theory, than metacognition. As you will read in a few paragraphs' time, metacognition has a very narrow focus, whereas self-regulation is the more general, or less specific, idea of how students control their emotions, monitor their motivations and show resilience with difficult problems. Though metacognition would fall under this umbrella, it would be incorrect to suggest that metacognition covers all of these areas.

What Metacognition Is

Through my years of research on metacognition, the definition that I have come across the most is that of 'thinking about thinking'. Though this definition begins to push us in the correct direction of understanding what metacognition is, it again is not hugely accurate or specific in understanding what metacognition *truly* is. The best definition that I have come across in literature is that from Flavell (1976), who wrote:

> I am being metacognitive if I notice that I am having more trouble learning A than B; if it strikes me that I should double check C before accepting it as fact.

This definition is perhaps still a little unclear, though – or at least it is until we begin to explore metacognitive theory in a bit more depth. When you have an understanding of the theory, this definition makes sense. But, really, a definition should make sense without a need to know the ins and outs of the theory. This led me to produce my own definition of metacognition, which is:

> The little voice inside your head that constantly evaluates and informs your actions.

What this definition is attempting to suggest is that metacognition is that consistent internal monologue that says, 'Do it like this, not like that', or 'That did not go as well as planned, I will do it like that next time'.

This, therefore, begins to bring us on to what metacognition truly is. The word itself can be broken down into two. First is meta, or the idea of 'higher order'. The second is cognition, or the idea of how we acquire and utilise knowledge. Therefore, metacognition is actually referring to the higher-order thinking around how we acquire and utilise our own knowledge. This allows us to reconsider the definitions that we have above, where metacognition is the consistent and repeated evaluation and review of our own learning, and how we are going about applying and utilising the knowledge that we have.

We are several paragraphs into this chapter, and you may be lost. Let us therefore consider some less abstract definitions, and settle on a fixed, concrete example that we will all have gone through in our lives – the drive to work.

Driving to work

Before: What is the quickest route to school? What might the impact of new traffic lights be? Do I need to change my route because of this? What time do I need to set off to ensure I am there on time?

During: How does this diversion impact on me? How will I correct my taking of the wrong road? Can I amend my route to make up for the traffic that I have just hit?

After: The traffic at this time of day is too bad to take route x. The new roadworks mean I will need to travel on route y. The corners on route z are quite tight, and so I need to take them slower next time.

The cognition of driving are the skills we have to drive and our abilities to adapt to the road conditions that we have in front of us. The metacognitive thinking is the review of the actions we take, including how we are driving and the routes we take.

It is perhaps no surprise that metacognition is so difficult to understand. If we consider the prerequisites of metacognition, which are cognition (as you cannot have higher-order consideration of cognition without cognition actually occurring) and motivation (as without this, cognition would not be used), these are both themselves visible. For example, cognition could be seen in the mirror of a dance studio or the videoing of a golf swing. Meanwhile, motivation becomes visible through witnessing the completion of a task, such as the handing in of a homework task or a student asking for a challenge worksheet. However, metacognition does not allow this visibility, which is even shown within the driving example given above. This is where the first key demand of this book comes. In order to develop our own metacognition, and the metacognitive abilities of our students, we need to make metacognition explicit, through active, conscious consideration of metacognitive practices, as well as through explicit reference within our teaching.

Knowledge of Cognition vs Regulation of Cognition

Now that we have an understanding (or the beginning of an understanding) of what metacognition is, it is time to explore the deep dark depths of the theory. Metacognition itself is split into two areas – knowledge of cognition and regulation of cognition.

- **Knowledge of cognition:** this refers to what we, as individuals, understand of our own cognition. This includes what we know about our levels of knowledge, including facts and strategies with which we have to approach tasks and problems. In short, this is what we know.
- **Regulation of cognition:** this refers to the ways in which we control and monitor our own thinking and learning. This would include evaluation of strategies and tasks that we have completed. In short, this is our ability to evaluate.

Once metacognition has been split down into these two areas, they are actually split down into three further areas. This is hugely important, as this provides us with something called the metacognitive processes. These processes are so important that they demand their own chapter of strategies later on in this book. In essence, these metacognitive processes are the engine room of metacognition. It is here where the proper metacognitive thinking will be occurring for ourselves and our students, and where we can make the biggest impacts on student metacognitive developments.

Let us first explore how knowledge of cognition is broken down:

Knowledge of self

- This refers to the factors which will impact on an individual's performance during a task, and is specifically in relation to the cognition that we can draw on to complete the task, including the knowledge that we have that is required by the task.
- Examples of knowledge of self can include:
  - o 'I do not know any key dates in relation to the Second World War.'
  - o 'I am confident about the stages of waterfall formation.'
  - o 'I can recall only two alternative shading techniques, but I know that there are more that I should be aware of in order to complete this task successfully.'

Knowledge of strategies

- This refers to our knowledge of alternative strategies that could be used to attempt and/or complete a task or problem, as well as a firm understanding of the correct stages to work through to successfully utilise a strategy.
- Examples of knowledge of strategies include:
  - o 'The first step is x, the second step is y.'
  - o 'I am going to use strategy w for this task, because ...'
  - o 'I do not think that strategy y would be appropriate for this task, because ...'

Knowledge of task

- This refers to our comprehension of the task that has been given to us, including what must be included in any answer.
- Examples of knowledge of task include:
  - o 'The task requires me to include ...'
  - o 'The questions suggest that I need to provide an answer in format x.'

Now, let us consider how regulation of cognition is broken down:

Planning

- This refers to the approaches that can be taken to plan for a task.
- Examples of this include:
  - What is the task requiring of me?
  - What strategies do I have available to me to attempt this task?
  - What content do I need to include within any answer or solution?
  - What layout does my answer need to take?

Monitoring

- This refers to the consistent evaluation of a solution or answer during its completion, to ensure that it is still in line with the plan produced and the task criteria laid out. The purpose of monitoring is to ensure that any changes to approach or changes to content already included within the answer are made before the final solution or answer is produced.
- Examples of this include:
  - 'How long do I have left to complete this task?'
  - 'Have I met all of the task criteria in my answer so far?'
  - 'Is the strategy or approach that I am taking to this task working? Am I moving towards a sensible answer or solution?'

Evaluation

- This refers to the conclusions drawn once an activity has been completed in order to review performance against the success criteria of the said activity.
- Examples of this include:
  - 'Did I successfully meet the task criteria that were outlined?'
  - 'Did the approach that I used for this activity work successfully? How do I know?'
  - 'How would I go about this task if I were to repeat it now?'

Translating Metacognitive Abilities

Though the metacognitive theory and how this is broken down into different areas should now be clear, it is important to understand how metacognitive abilities reside within us and get developed. The first crucial point here is on our ability to translate metacognitive abilities from one area to another.

In short, metacognitive abilities cannot be transferred from one area to another. Let us reconsider the definition of metacognition, which is the higher-order thinking of a cognitive action. Therefore, the 'meta' is linked to the 'cognition'. Where the cognition varies, so does the 'meta' aspect. Not only does this mean that the metacognitive skills that a student may have mastered within, for example, English may not transfer to mathematics, it also means that they may not transfer from one topic to another topic, for example from poem interpretations to persuasive writing. This is because cognition is not just subject specific, but it is also topic specific.

Unfortunately, this raises a huge issue for us. This means that we cannot ever presume that a student's previous metacognitive strengths will be translated from one topic to the next, and therefore we would need to assess these abilities once again. However, there is a light at the end of the tunnel. Though the meta varies on the cognition, many of the metacognitive approaches that we need students to be aware of and utilise do not vary by cognition, and so, although these metacognitive skills may not always be at the same level for all topics, they will still be there. In effect, students will not be resetting to 'zero' metacognitive skill at the beginning of each topic. Let us take the example of evaluation. A strong metacognitive practitioner will be aware that they need to review their practice at the end of each task or activity that they complete. This may involve analysing the effectiveness and speed of the strategy used, reviewing their comprehension of the task versus a mark scheme and the reconsideration of knowledge of self. These are approaches that this strong metacognitive practitioner would take regardless of the cognition. Yes, there may be more specific and alternative questions that need to be asked that vary with the cognition, but there will always be a base level of effective 'meta' practice that can be drawn upon regardless of the topic area. So, how does this impact on us? We need to train students up metacognitively, so that they hold strong metacognitive approaches regardless. However, with each new topic, we need to assess and develop each student's metacognition within that topic area specifically, to ensure that students have both the general and specific metacognitive approaches that they require to be successful.

Metacognitive Levels

When reviewing metacognitive abilities of either ourselves or our learners, it is useful to have a framework within which to judge. In-depth assessments of student metacognitive abilities are highly complex things, which are not required for successful metacognitive implementation at a teacher level. However, it is useful for us to be able to provide a snapshot of where students are with their metacognitive abilities, which is where Perkins' (1992) 'levels of metacognition' provide us with the perfect framework. Perkins defines four levels – tacit, aware, strategic and reflective – which can be defined as below:

Tacit – students are going through the cognitive processes, but they are not aware/conscious of this and no metacognitive thought is being actively considered.

Aware – students begin to become aware of their cognitive evaluation, but this is still fairly muddled and disorganised (i.e. there is not a strategic metacognitive approach occurring, merely the beginnings of metacognitive thought).

Strategic – students are considering their metacognition on a more regular basis, in a more organised manner, using implicit strategies.

Reflective – students are consistently reflecting upon their own practice, not just following the completion of a cognitive action, but also during (monitoring). Metacognitive thoughts are conscious, organised and frequent.

Unfortunately, most students will be towards the tacit side of this scale (or sometimes it seems like they are not even here, where cognitive actions are not taking place). Though this may seem a depressing thought – students are so metacognitively poor generally – it does of course mean that there is more opportunity for us to add positive impact to students' learning and development. The more that they need to improve their metacognition, the more that we will be able to help them.

The Rationale for Metacognition

The purpose of this section is to present to you the best evidence and research that is out there on metacognition to prove to you that it is just as beneficial as I believe it is. Hopefully, the evidence that is shown below will give you the confidence that this really is something that is worth investing in, rather than some new dud that will disappear within a few years, or a wishy-washy theory which does not really apply to the classroom and should be ignored.

In order to make this evidence as clear as possible, findings from different research papers will be summarised, presenting you with the key headlines from some of the most significant papers on metacognition over the previous century. There will also be summaries of comments from the Education Endowment Foundation (EEF) and the Office for Standards in Education (Ofsted), both of whom are very supportive of the benefits of developing teachers' and schools' metacognitive practices.

EEF

The EEF is the go-to place for high-quality summaries on educational theories, including that on metacognition. In 2018, the EEF published a superbly accessible report on metacognition, produced after years of literature reviews by academics far cleverer than me! What you may already know about EEF reports is that they provide a numerical value for the impact of implementing a certain policy or pedagogical practices, in terms of months. Though I take these values with a pinch of salt (quite how a new pedagogical approach will lead to 'x' months improvements, I am not sure), this measure of months does provide us with a way to compare the relative impact of different interventions. At the time of writing, the EEF does not have a pedagogical approach or intervention that is *more* effective than metacognition, which has an improvement rating of seven months.

Furthermore, the EEF consider this judgement to be 'four padlocks', which in layman's terms means that the evidence is sound. This is later backed up by a 2020 evidence report, again by the EEF, which goes through the literature over the course of 60-plus pages, again concluding that the benefits of metacognitive practice are significant.

Ofsted

Over recent years, Ofsted have made the move towards being more evidence informed. Therefore, it is unsurprising to find out that they consider metacognitive practice as something that teaching professionals should be aware of and be developing. In their 2019 overview of research document, which details different high-quality and research-proven pedagogies staff should be encountering and developing during staff training, metacognition is one of those areas. Of course, we should not just do things in our school because they are what Ofsted say we should do. However, when we have a teaching and learning strategy that has such strong evidence on its positive impacts, *and* Ofsted details how metacognition should be a pedagogy covered by a successful continuous professional development (CPD) programme, then it really is a win–win situation.

Kuhn (1989)

Kuhn has completed significant quantities of research around the development of metacognition, including particularly interesting research around the ages that students can acquire metacognitive skills. Her 1989 research reached the conclusion that the metacognitive development of individuals between their early teenage years and adulthood is either only very slightly improved, or no change has been recorded. Equally, this research found that individuals who were in educational settings developed their own metacognitive abilities at a faster rate than those who were not in educational settings (or even that those in educational settings improved their metacognitive skills whilst those not in educational did not improve their metacognitive skills at all). Two clear conclusions can be drawn out here. Firstly, education is the gateway to drive metacognitive development – i.e. it is our job. Secondly, this research shows that were we just to leave metacognition to develop on its own, this development is either very slow or non-existent. This, therefore, is more evidence that points towards us, at the coal-face of education, as being the ones who need to support student metacognitive development.

Callan et al. (2016)

The paper explored the implications of social groupings, and how this can contribute to levels of metacognitive skill. Within this research, it was found that white British students used metacognitive strategies fewer than *any* other grouping of students based upon their ethnicity. Of course, not all UK secondary schools are majority white British; however, the majority of UK secondary school students *are* white British.

This therefore provides a situation where the majority of schools contain a majority of students from a grouping where metacognitive strategies are used more infrequently than any other group of students. If we consider the silver lining on this, however, it is once again that this provides us with the opportunity to provide more 'added value' for each student.

Willingham (2011)

In his summary on metacognition, Willingham provides an extremely compelling case for the use of the theory in schools. Willingham details in this research that students who have higher self-regulatory abilities (recalling that metacognition is a part of self-regulation) have improved school readiness, have higher predicted reading and maths proficiency, and also have a reduced likelihood of expulsion (probably due to the other factors detailed). So, in short, those with metacognition skills will be better at the two gateway skills required for all subjects – reading and mathematics.

Teong (2003)

In this study, the ability of students to problem solve (including tackling and completing problem solving) was assessed. Teong found that 'novice' problem solvers lacked metacognitive skills including the ability to monitor their work, assess the work that they had completed and review the cognitive strategies that they had utilised to attempt the problem. Within the study, students were trained up with only *one* metacognitive strategy. Following the cementing of this strategy in student practice, students were reassessed, and were shown to have outperformed students who did not receive the metacognitive training (i.e. it was the metacognitive training that supported the students' improved outcomes). Equally, and importantly for our own classroom practice, the research showed that low prior attainment (LPA) students also improved their own metacognitive abilities within this training, leading to more regulated answers. This provides crucial evidence in showing that metacognition can be utilised with all students, and not just the more able or 'cognitively advanced'.

Toth et al. (2000); Zohar and Ben-David (2008); Ben-David and Zohar (2009)

These three separate studies all provided similar impacts to each other, and similarly positive outcomes to the work by Teong (2003). In each of these studies, students developed a metacognitive area, in these scenarios named meta-strategic knowledge (MSK). The focus of MSK is to choose the most appropriate strategy for a given task or problem. This intervention led to superb outcomes, with students significantly improving their strategic and meta-strategic thinking. These findings were also true for LPA students, as well as high prior attaining (HPA) students.

Mevarech and Kramarski (1997); Mevarech (1999); Kramarski et al. (2002); Mevarech and Amrany (2008)

You will begin to notice a certain theme with the references within this book. Many references are in relation to work done by the remarkable academic Mevarech. The work, often complemented by Kramarski, provides further insights into the benefits of metacognitive instruction. Focusing on problem solving, in particular in the field of mathematics, each of these studies concluded that (mathematical) problem solving was significantly improved following the roll-out of tweaked teacher delivery. This tweaked teacher delivery included a focus on a metacognition, unsurprisingly, and had wonderful impacts on students. These studies found that LPA, HPA and middle prior attainers (MPA) all made progress due to this type of metacognitive teaching. Moreover, these findings were repeated by Onu et al. (2012), showing they work for academics other than Mevarech, too.

The rationale for metacognition – real-life practice

As well as the academia providing the evidence we need to implement metacognition in our schools, there are also real-life case studies that provide us with evidence, too. Below, Rachel Cliffe describes the metacognitive project that she ran and the positive outcomes it achieved:

> As part of the Chartered Teacher qualification, I undertook a research project in 2021 which evaluated the use of a metacognitive exam question grid with GCSE History students. The aim was to evaluate the impact of the grid on Year 9 students' assessment performance and perceptions of performance using a sample from a research and control group. The data was measured using a baseline and end of project assessment and a questionnaire to examine perceptions. The sample students were chosen using a ratified random sample approach which matched their ability across the research and control group. The decision to use a sample was due to the ability of the groups – a direct comparison would not have been effective as one group had a greater number of higher-prior attaining (HPA) students. It must be noted that both groups are taught by myself and the only difference in lessons across the project was the metacognitive grid (and a fire drill).
>
> The project found that across the sample of 12 students, the HPA students in the research group using the grid made greater progress between the baseline and end of project assessment than the HPA students in the control group. Furthermore, the Likert quantitative data suggested that the metacognition grid in the research group had a positive impact on students' perceptions of their exam performance and that they felt more confident with structuring exam questions, their progress with GCSE exam questions and were more aware of

their areas to improve for each exam question style. The most significant gap was an awareness of how to improve 10-mark exam questions with the average research group sample (6 students) score of 4.2 compared to the control group sample (6 students) of 3.5 – with 5 being the highest rating. Although the sample was small, the results of the project suggest that the metacognitive exam question grid had a positive impact on the students' perceptions of performance and progress across a short period of time. The next steps are to embed the grid over a longer period of time across both groups and examine the articulation of metacognition and the impact of socioeconomic status on metacognition.

Julie Copping has also conducted metacognitive research, in particular looking at students' increased progress following effective metacognitive questioning (see case study below).

Metacognitive questioning in religious education (RE)

At my college, we have formed a dynamic learning community. Teachers are provided with the right support, time and training in small coaching groups to complete a research project which will develop their practice. This year our focus has been *feedback and metacognition*.

Over the last academic year, I have been researching how effective metacognitive questioning can improve students' ability to self-regulate their learning and make better progress.

Throughout the year I have prompted students to think more deeply about their work. The results have been very rewarding. A poster of key questions was produced. It has been reviewed and adapted throughout the year following a continuous cycle of formative feedback, summative assessments and student feedback.

Students have focussed on the skills of describe, explain and evaluate in every unit. This is to develop their application of the skills and understand how they are transferable across each unit. The skills ladder outlines how they can progress the skills from Years 7–9.

Below is an example from a Year 7 'explain' task:

Baseline autumn term 'explain' answer

Q: 'Explain how the Church unites the Christian community and the five pillars unite the Muslim community.'

A: 'The five pillars unite Muslims because it is a way to show that they are all Muslims and they all go through the same thing. The five pillars are made to show that they all follow Allah. The Church unites Christians because they all believe in the same god and pray to the same person. The thing that makes them all Christians is the god they believe in. All of Christians pray and worship and change their lifestyles to be a Christian. All Muslims worship Allah and Muhammad is his messenger. The five pillars are rules to follow that they all do.'

The answer demonstrates some surface-level knowledge but lacks depth and does not follow the expected structure of an 'explain' answer. When she received her feedback and looked again at her answer, she made the following reflections:

> I would have liked to achieve higher than skill 5, I was hoping for a 7 or 8. I needed to stop going on and get to the point. I know how to do this now. I can see how to improve. I should have included more facts and key words in my answer too.

Summative assessment spring term 'explain' answer

Q: 'Explain how a Hindu may perform their dharma.'

A: 'Dharma means duty and it is a Hindu's duty to fulfil their dharma throughout their life. To follow dharma, a Hindu must live out and follow the dharma that matches the lives they are given. For example, in the caste system, you start off low down; if you follow your duties, you will be reincarnated higher up the caste system. If you are in the Sudra caste you will do a hard-working manual job. If you are born into the warrior caste you will fight to protect others.

'Doing your dharma is important to a Hindu because if you do your dharma, you will get good karma and escape samsara (the circle of life and death). Hindus follow dharma in the same way that Muslims follow the five pillars of Islam. Hindus work towards escaping samsara and achieving Moksha.'

As you can see, there has been clear progress. She is attempting to make a point, provide examples and explain their importance. She is also using more key words. Overall, her answer shows more depth of knowledge. She was able to reflect on her work and explain what she would need to do to move up the skills ladder. What was particularly pleasing was the way she was referring to the skills ladder throughout the assessment, ticking off skills and editing her work as she went. It was great to see this level of awareness, self-regulation, and motivation.

Julie Copping – Lead Practitioner for Teaching and Learning

Further Reading

The following weblinks will provide you with blogs and booklets that provide further readings on metacognitive theory:

Beach, P. T., Anderson, R.C., Jacovidis, J. N. and Chadwick, K. K. (2020). 'Making the Abstract Explicit: The Role of Metacognition in Teaching and Learning', Inflexion – Policy Paper, available at: https://www.inflexion.org/making-the-abstract-explicit-the-role-of-metacognition-in-teaching-and-learning/ (accessed 4 May 2022)

Bromley, M. (2018). 'In the Classroom: Metacognition Explained', SecEd, available at: www.sec-ed.co.uk/best-practice/in-the-classroom-metacognition-explained/ (accessed 4 May 2022)

Cambridge Assessment International Education (2019). 'Metacognition', Teaching & Learning Team, Cambridge International, available at: https://cambridge-community.org.uk/professional-development/gswmeta/index.html (accessed 4 May 2022)

EEF (2021). 'Metacognition and Self-Regulated Learning', Educational Endowment Foundation, available at: https://educationendowmentfoundation.org.uk/tools/guidance-reports/metacognition-and-self-regulated-learning/ (accessed 4 May 2022)

EEF (2021). 'Metacognition and Self-Regulation', Educational Endowment Foundation, available at: https://educationendowmentfoundation.org.uk/evidence-summaries/teaching-learning-toolkit/meta-cognition-and-self-regulation/ (accessed 4 May 2022)

2
Myths of Metacognition

Learning Objectives

In this chapter we will:

- Explore the four main misconceptions around metacognition
- Understand why these are misconceptions
- Discuss how to prevent these misconceptions from drifting into your teaching practice.

Introduction

So far, this book has explored the theory behind metacognition, as well as the justification for introducing metacognitive teaching into our classrooms. However, one area that this book has so far not touched upon is that of common misconceptions around metacognition. Though many misconceptions around metacognition revolve around a definition, a confusion with self-regulation and discrete teaching of skills, there are also key misconceptions that have arisen around when metacognition should be introduced into the classroom.

These misconceptions revolve around the age, gender and academic ability of students, and are as follows:

1   Metacognition is only for high-attaining students.
2   Metacognition is not for students with special educational needs (SEN).
3   Metacognition is only for older students.
4   Metacognition is only for girls.

Hopefully, you will see these misconceptions and already realise how ridiculous they are. However, it is crucial that time is taken to explore these misconceptions, how they have arisen and why they are wrong. If you are going to ensure that you are effectively developing your metacognitive understanding and are accurately introducing and developing it in your classroom, then you will need to be aware of these key misconceptions.

Metacognition Is Only for Higher-Attaining Students

The first misconception that is going to be explored is around the academic ability of students and how these impact on their ability to engage with metacognition. From my experiences, reading of blogs and general immersion within the world of metacognition, I have observed that unfortunately there is a large group of educational professionals who believe that metacognition and metacognitive strategies should only be used with students that we identify as higher attaining or most able.

Though it is very easy to be critical of this – all students should of course be given the opportunity to improve themselves as learners, and it is unfair to write them off just because they are 'low ability' – there is some rationale for this misconception. As explained in the first chapter in this book, metacognition is built from an individual's cognition – that is the range of cognitive abilities and strategies that they have to attempt a task. Where students do not have the cognition – that is, subject knowledge – they are going to struggle significantly with metacognitive aspects. Where students do not have a command of subject knowledge, they are going to struggle to be able to start to evaluate strategies, consider what knowledge they have and what areas they need to be working on. These students are going to struggle to deal with modelling of multiple different strategies when they have yet to master just one, and are going to be unable to then discuss the effectiveness of each strategy within a group discussion.

Therefore, where metacognition is reliant upon a student's cognitive ability, it does make some sense that metacognitive strategies, and developing student metacognition, will be easier with those students whom we identify as higher ability. Where students have a good grounding in the subject content, where students are confident using a range of strategies, and can begin to consider the effectiveness and appropriateness of a range of strategies, consider their own strengths and weaknesses, and so forth, they are of course going to be in a far better position to begin to develop their metacognition even further. Furthermore, it is true that students who are higher attaining are more likely to have higher metacognitive abilities already. Therefore, this 'harder' thinking will not be too much for these students. These ideas are backed up by the literature too, with Rami and Govil (2013) concluding that it is higher-achieving students who utilise metacognitive strategies more frequently than students who are not identified as high achieving. Artzz and Armour-Thomas (1992) explore these ideas too, and again found that students who were more successful at mathematical problem solving utilise metacognitive strategies to a greater extent. Both of these pieces of research back up where this misconception may come from, then, as does research by Kramarski, Mevarech and Arami (2002), which found that lower prior attaining (LPA) students utilised fewer metacognitive strategies to tackle problems, and were also more unsuccessful than non-LPA students in completing, or at least working through, these problems.

However, not only is it unethical not to delve into metacognition with 'lower-ability' students just because they are 'lower ability', it is also pedagogically wrong. Do we not teach students key knowledge because they are 'lower ability'? Majoritively, no.

(Of course, students will study different things in certain subjects, depending on their setting or ability levels, but typically all students will learn all topics.) Where students are struggling, we simply provide some level of scaffolding. This may be additional modelling, it may be a knowledge organiser, a teaching assistant (TA) or some other form of support, but we do support these students in order to access the work. The same is completely true of metacognition. There is absolutely no reason why students who are 'lower ability' cannot develop their metacognition. It may just be that they begin to develop it a little later into a topic, when they have mastered more of the new subject content, and/or it may be that these students just require a little more scaffolding than other students.

Furthermore, it is impossible to accurately identify higher, middle and lower attainers effectively. It is even more impossible to do this lesson by lesson, topic by topic and subject by subject. Metacognitive abilities will vary for a student from subject to subject and topic to topic. It would be impossible for a teacher to assess this every single time. Therefore, are you going to just forget about metacognition altogether, despite the incredible benefits it can bring to your students, or are you just going to develop it in all students, and have appropriate scaffolding and support available for those students who are struggling, much as you would for students struggling to pick up specific subject content?

Dangerously, this misconception (much as the others, actually) becomes somewhat of a self-fulfilling prophecy. If a teacher determines that a student is unable to develop their metacognitive abilities (for whatever reason), they will then not provide these students with the opportunity to develop their metacognition. If this student is not provided with the opportunity to develop their metacognition, then their metacognition is not going to improve, and actually they will never be able to access metacognitive strategies or develop their metacognition effectively. This self-fulfilling prophecy is true of all content, though. If a teacher determines that a student is, for example, not able to effectively spell place names and they never take the time to correct these mistakes, then that student is not suddenly going to magically know how to spell the place names accurately.

Metacognition Is Not for Students with SEN

Similarly, to the previous misconception, there is a belief that students with SEN are unable to be metacognitive and to access metacognitive strategies. Once again, this misconception arises from a mistaken belief that SEN students are not able or not sufficiently academic enough to be able to access or attempt this higher-order thinking. It also revolves around the incorrect belief that all SEN students also should not be pushed and challenged, and so they do not need to approach something as complicated as metacognition. These are of course very antiquated views that hopefully are no longer prevalent (or existing what-so-ever) within our profession. However, they have existed, and so we need to be aware of them. Once again, no students, regardless of their prior abilities or the support that they may need, should be prevented from developing their metacognitive thinking. Of course, scaffolds will need to be put into place, but this is true of all students, and certainly not a reason for failing to allow our SEN students to develop their metacognitive abilities.

However, as a curveball, there are considerations that we may need to take for our SEN students, depending on their specific situations, when we are looking to support their metacognitive development. For example, where students have working memory difficulties, and cannot process as much information at once, it would be unfair to expect that student to be able to monitor their work as they are actually producing it. Rather, greater emphasis, for this type of student, would need to be placed on successful evaluation (and future planning) following the competition of the task. Additionally, some students may struggle working in the cacophony of a group discussion situation, or may need to work one-to-one with a TA, which again would need to be considered when a discussion task was being planned and utilised within a lesson.

Schools have terrific SEN set-ups these days, and the information that your SENCO and their team will have on each pupil will be vast. Most schools also provide passports/one-page documents on students that they share with class teachers as an overview on a student. If you are concerned about how a metacognitive task may work with SEN students in your classes, then consider these documents, and if you are still concerned about the suitability of a strategy, or any scaffolds that would be required for a student, then try to take the time to speak to your special educational needs co-ordinator (SENCo) and/or their team. You will find that each strategy within this book is clearly explained, both as to what it is and how it works. This should provide the information that you need to support a conversation with members of the SEN team about a specific strategy and the requirements of particular students.

Just remember, the overall aim is to ensure that all students get the opportunity to develop their metacognitive skillset, even if this means tweaking, changing and scaffolding the strategies that you are going to be using in your lessons.

Metacognition Is Only for Older Students

It seems likely that the misconception that only older students can be metacognitive arises from a similar train of thought to that of the misconception surrounding only higher-ability students being able to demonstrate and develop their metacognition. As metacognition is an abstract theory, and something that can be quite difficult not only to explain, but provide examples for, it suddenly becomes something that we perceive only older individuals, or maybe adults, would be able to get their heads around.

However, and unsurprisingly given the nature of this paragraph, this is an incorrect myth. As Kuhn (1989) discovered, metacognition is actually displayed by individuals as young as two. Let us consider this example. My son, at this point almost two years old, was knocking pegs through holes. He was doing this with a wooden hammer, and began knocking the pegs with the curved side of the hammer. However, this was not having the desired effect, as the pegs were either not going through, or going through only ever so slightly, as the hammer slipped off the top of the peg with each impact. He then took some time to assess the hammer, and then decided to twist it around, so that he was hitting the pegs with the flat side. The impact was instant, as the pegs got hit through straight away. Now, I am not claiming that my twenty-odd-month-old was explicitly thinking, 'Ah yes, let me be metacognitive about this'. However, he probably was thinking something along the lines of, 'Hmm, this is not working quite as a planned, so why not try it the other way around and see if I have more success whacking these things that way?' And this, in itself, is metacognition.

The question still remains, though, that if individuals are metacognitive at such a young age, but do not really understand what is going on, is there really any point being metacognitive with them? We also have to question whether a group that is struggling with subject content, whether they are a weak Year 7 class or a top-set Year 11 class, should really be considering metacognition or whether they should just crack on with the content. My argument is this: metacognition is always there. Where cognition is occurring, metacognition is happening in the background. Equally, the more metacognitive that we are, the more effective we will be in our reflections, in our purposeful practice, and the more effective we will be with problem solving. There is a string of reasons, as outlined in the previous chapter, as to why metacognition is important. Therefore, yes, we are not going to be explicitly metacognitive with a 20-month-old. However, it is clearly important for us to begin developing metacognition at the youngest age that we possibly can. The sooner that we begin addressing metacognition, the sooner advances are made. For example, we do not wait until secondary school to start teaching mathematics. Mathematics is in the world around us and, actually, kids will have some grasp of numbers, patterns and shapes before they are even enrolled in full-time education. Again, though, we introduce mathematics in an age-appropriate way. We are not going to whip out the quadratic formula for a bunch of Year 1 students, nor are we going to look at number bonds for a good group of Key Stage 5 students. It is all about what is appropriate, considering we know that the area of development, whether that be mathematics or metacognition, is crucial to develop.

So, in conclusion to this myth, it is true that young individuals would not understand the abstract concept of metacognition. If we are being honest, it is quite difficult to understand as a well-educated adult. However, metacognition is intrinsically linked with each and every cognitive action. It exists in all individuals, of all ages, regardless of ability. Therefore, we need to be developing metacognitive skills in students from day dot.

Metacognition Is Only for Girls

The myth around metacognition being only for girls is an interesting one. It is one that I have heard a handful of times, but does have a bit of support within general literature.

Topca and Yilmaz-Tuzun (2009) detailed in their research that girls were more likely than boys to utilise metacognitive strategies. However, this was challenged in work by Rami and Govil (2013) who did not draw the same conclusions on metacognitive skills, usage and gender. Therefore, it raises the question of where this myth may have arisen from. I have two ideas on this. Firstly, I wonder if it comes from the idea, or rather the misconception, of what effective revision looks like? The teaching profession is hopefully clear now on the limited value of highlighting and writing out pages and pages of revision notes. These just are not good ways to revise effectively. Yet, I know when I was at school that these were the ways that we were expected to revise, and typically (or rather, stereotypically) girls had far neater notes than boys, with pretty highlighting throughout (this really is a troubling misconception, too). As these notes were nicer, clearer, prettier, this revision was deemed superior, and therefore girls were better at revising. I presume this has then linked in with misconstrued ideas of metacognition, and where girls were producing pretty revision notes, they must be the ones who could be metacognitive themselves. However, hopefully be reading this far into the book, you are clear that this just is not true.

I also wonder whether a misconception has arisen due to the difficulty of metacognition. As we know, it is abstract and quite difficult to comprehend. We most certainly could not sit down with a class of students and try to go through all of the theory, and be expecting them to follow, or even be awake, by the end of the lesson. Equally, metacognition requires deeper and harder thinking, which again, I think, may lead into the idea that metacognition is a girl's skill, where girls are able to think deeper and think harder (perhaps backed up with superior GCSE grades for girls, and the chronic issue surrounding boys underachieving in the UK). Again, this just is not true. What is true, and would be fair to say, is that students who are going to be successful metacognitively do need to grasp the subject content that they are dealing with. They also need to be resilient – and be able to continue working where they are stuck or it gets a bit difficult. Any stereotyping that associates this with girls, rather than boys, is just incorrect. But again, it might provide some reasoning as to where this myth has stemmed from.

So, overall, the claim of boys not being able to develop their metacognition and it being a girl-only thing is completely false.

You may find that on your metacognitive journey, especially as you read more or speak to colleagues, you find yourself facing these myths, or perhaps others. Hopefully, through having read through the theory, the rationale for introducing metacognition, as well as these four myths above, you will feel as if you have ammunition to tackle these misconceptions and myths. Even if you do not, at least you know what is fact and what is fiction. Equally, if you do find out reasons for these misconceptions, please let me know. Much of the above is taken from conversations, readings and anecdotes. There is little to no research on metacognitive myths, so perhaps you could be the one who finds out more.

Summary

- There are four significant myths surrounding metacognition. These are that metacognition is only for able students, older students, non-SEN students and girl students. These are all completely false.
- Metacognition is intrinsically linked to cognition, which is something that we all do every single day. Therefore, we are all metacognitive.
- Many of these myths do not appear to have clear origins or significant research into them. However, we do have the evidence to show the reason why metacognition is so important and why it is for all.

Further Reading

To consider more myths of metacognition, check out:

Burns, N. (2021). '5 Myths about Metacognition that We Need to Banish', *Tes*, available at: www.tes.com/magazine/archived/5-myths-about-metacognition-we-need-banish (accessed 4 May 2022)

InnerDrive (2022). '4 Misconceptions about Metacognition', InnerDrive, available at: https://blog.innerdrive.co.uk/4-misconceptions-about-metacognition (accessed 4 May 2022)

Whitebread, D. and Coltman, P. (2010). 'Aspects of Pedagogy Supporting Metacognition and Self-Regulation in Mathematical Learning of Young Children: Evidence from an Observational Study', *ZDM Mathematics Education*, 42, pp. 163–178.

3
Metacognitive Processes

Learning Objectives

In this chapter we will:

- Explore the importance of metacognitive processes
- Consider how metacognitive processes can be made visible in the classroom with a variety of different strategies.

Introduction

As discussed in Chapter 1, metacognitive processes are incredibly important within the classroom. A century worth of research has been broken down into the planning, monitoring and evaluation, and the 'Knowledge of' cycles, which should inform our teaching as well as our learning.

So, what are we looking for when bringing metacognitive processes into the classroom? The key point here, as it will be whenever metacognitive strategies are mentioned, is about making our thinking explicit. It was explored how metacognition consists of the processes of planning, monitoring and evaluation, as well as knowledge of self, knowledge of task and knowledge of strategies. As experts, we have spent years working through these cycles and honing our expertise. Take the average lesson, for example. We may, at some point, quite likely in our early years of teaching, have produced a clear lesson plan, alongside printed resources and a fancy looking PowerPoint. We would then have taught that lesson, monitoring as we taught it to ensure that students were learning and that we were moving towards our desired objectives or learning goals. Following the lesson, we would then have reviewed how much progress was made in that lesson, considered where we would be starting the next lesson from, and also considering what went well, and what did not, in that lesson, as well as considering what we would do better next time. As the years move on, and we teach that lesson over and over again, the formal lesson plan probably goes, as may some of the resources. But each time we teach that lesson, we are building on prior experience, and learning more about how to, and how not to, teach that topic to students. As teachers, we are incredible at going through these cycles multiple times a day, in a range of different scenarios, such as the lesson example just given, or in the way we conduct meetings, have conversations with upset students or deal with a safeguarding issue. Of course, we do not need to share our expertise with students on these areas, but we do need to consider how we can make these processes explicit to students. How can we ensure that students are actually planning, monitoring and evaluating? How can we ensure that students are considering knowledge of self, knowledge of task and knowledge of strategies? We know that if students are doing this, they will be more effective independent learners. They will have a sensible and effective cycle to go through when completing tasks. They will be considering previous successes and learning from mistakes. These students will be considering their content knowledge – especially gaps – as well as their understanding of strategies available to them, and any help that they may need. If we, as effective workers and learners, are going through these stages, then so should our students.

This chapter will explore the ways that we can seamlessly integrate metacognitive processes into our lessons. The first of five strategies will be that of modelling.

Modelling

What

As teachers, we are expert metacognitive practitioners, even if we are not aware of our own metacognition. Specifically, we are experts in the use of metacognitive processes such as planning, monitoring and evaluating. This strategy places an emphasis on shining a light on this thinking by modelling it to students as we would with any other strategy or new content that we desire them to learn. This could either be done discretely, or it could be embedded within your usual modelling format, with a few new phrases and explanations thrown in.

When/How

It is possible to model the metacognitive processes both within your typical modelling, or discretely too, with examples addressed below. Over time, it would be wise to begin to incorporate this explanation, and the discussion that comes with it, within your current modelling, to avoid both the feeling that the metacognitive process modelling is a bolt-on, and to ensure that it is being discussed seamlessly and appropriately, as opposed to a theoretical add-in. This strategy can be used, and even *should* be used, in every single lesson. We need to consistently shine a light on our thinking.

Why

Modelling is the key to every single lesson that we teach. Without high-quality modelling, students would not be able to learn new content or observe the use of new strategies.

We spend hours refining the way we will discuss a key concept, identify the key parts of a strategy or draw out the nuisances of a new planning tool, so why wouldn't we do the same for our metacognitive modelling? Modelling is so important, in fact, that it commands its own chapter later on within this book. But for now, modelling remains an incredibly powerful technique to support us, as the expert, in making our own metacognitive thinking explicit to our students. As with any learning, we need our students to understand the why, and not just the how. With regards to metacognition, and specifically metacognitive processes, it would be impossible for students to 'rote-learn' the processes. Rather, students need to understand the fundamentals of what we are doing. Therefore, through taking the time to share our own expert metacognitive thoughts, and to model them in a clear and precise way, students will begin to pick up on the type of thinking that goes on in our heads, and the ways that we utilise both the plan, monitor and evaluate cycle, and the knowledge of self, knowledge of task and knowledge of strategies cycle.

Examples

I am teaching students how to approach the analysis of a poem. I conduct my modelling as usual, going through the poem, drawing out key words, making notes and drawing up a plan for my answer, before writing out the answer, and then ensuring that I have covered all points. Following this, I could then provide a commentary to students along the lines of:

> You will have noticed that initially I took time to plan my response, drawing out key words and phrases that held particular power – for their meaning or suggested meaning – as well as planning my answer. I did this to ensure that I covered all points in my response to the question. When I started writing, I kept checking back to ensure I was following my plan – which is monitoring to make sure I am staying on track. Finally, I evaluated my work by cross-checking my answer with my plan, as well as with the question to make sure that I had met all of the question requirements.

By doing this, students understand the metacognitive processes that I have gone through in the piece of work that I have just modelled, and understand the benefits it will have for them if they also consciously consider those three parts when completing their own work, too.

Summary

- Be aware of the two main metacognitive cycles:
    - Knowledge of task, knowledge of self, knowledge of strategies;
    - Plan, monitor, evaluate.
- Make explicit reference to these cycles when modelling.
- Explain to students why you are moving through the different parts of the cycles.

Lesson Segmentation

What

This strategy places focus on breaking lessons up in accordance with the metacognitive process that you are following. This would mean breaking the lesson up into three parts, most likely of equal length, focusing on each of the three areas of each metacognitive process. Very much like a lesson having a starter, a main independent task and then a plenary, this type of lesson would focus on the planning of a task, monitoring whilst completing it and then evaluating a final answer; or, alternatively, would focus on identifying knowledge of self, before moving onto knowledge of task and lastly knowledge of strategies. This lesson segmentation may of course not take up the whole lesson, depending on the task, or it may be spread across multiple lessons. Equally, you may continue to have a do now and plenary task to maintain the crucial routine within your lessons.

When/How

Lesson segmentation is unlikely to be a strategy that is used every lesson, or even every week. Rather, it is a strategy that would be brought out when an explicit teaching point was needing to be made, such as essay writing, or possibly in the run-up to formal assessments and examinations, in order to ensure that students were clear with the processes that they should be going through. Equally, the knowledge cycle lends itself nicely to the revision of a unit, allowing students to evaluate everything that they have learnt or, equally, everything that they still need to learn prior to an assessment or an exam.

Why

The purpose of lesson segmentation is to make the metacognitive processes as explicit to students as possible. This is as close as you could possibly get to hitting students in the face with the cycles. Sometimes, when students just do not grasp something, we need to take away all subtlety in our delivery, and just make the point as explicitly as we can. That is the complete purpose of this strategy. Where students are still failing to follow the plan, monitor and evaluate cycle, or where students still are not considering factors in the knowledge cycle, then lesson segmentation could be utilised to make these processes incredibly explicit to students. This strategy therefore allows you to continue to reinforce student understanding of these processes (and we do need these cycles to become automatic in students sooner rather than later). It will also allow you to identify which students are already comfortable with going through these metacognitive stages, and which students are going to require further scaffolding, additional support and consistent reminders to incorporate these cycles into their thinking and day-to-day work.

Examples

Situation 1: I have just come to the end of a history topic with students, where considerable time has been spent identifying possible ways to include evidence within answers. To ensure that students have a clear understanding of the stages they need to go through, I provide students with a key question: 'Describe the causes of the Second World War, making reference to key dates and events.' Students are then instructed to write down on mini-whiteboards their knowledge of self for this question, their knowledge of task and their knowledge of strategies. By circulating the room, I am able to establish which students are conscious of the stages they need to go through when attempting a question like this one, and which students are unsure of one or more of the parts of the process.

Situation 2: I have recently spent time with a class listening to different pieces of music and identifying the different instruments that are being used. It became clear to me that students were not planning, monitoring and evaluating their work, as they were failing to identify many, if any, instruments correctly. To ensure that students had an approach for this type of task, I broke the lesson down into four sections. The first three sections focussed on students identifying a plan for the activity (how they were going to make notes, what were they listening for and so on), methods to monitor their progress (a list of instruments they knew couldn't come up so they shouldn't include) and then methods to evaluate (pair share, utilising posters, using up a clue card). Following this, in section four, students repeated the task several times, ensuring that they were planning, monitoring and evaluating their work for each new piece of music.

Summary

- Consider splitting your lesson into the three parts of either metacognitive cycle.
- Explicitly go through the different parts of the process for a given task or problem so that students are clear on the need to go through each part in turn.
- This strategy provides explicit practice for students with each part of the metacognitive cycles.

Worksheet Graphics

What

The worksheet graphic is a very simple strategy that merely involves placing a visual graphic of the cycle that you want students to engage with on the media that they are utilising. This may be a worksheet, a version that they glue into their books or something that appears on each slide on your PowerPoint presentation.

When/How

Extremely simple to do, there is never really an occasion where it would not be reasonable to include a cycle, or both cycles, within the media that students are utilising within that lesson. This is especially true of PowerPoints, where it is very straightforward to repeat the same graphic on each new slide. Furthermore, it would be possible for the part of the cycle that you are placing a focus on, for example 'monitoring', to show up in bold on the slide.

Why

Before considering why this is beneficial, it is incredibly important to note that by putting a static cycle on some worksheets learning will not improve. Metacognitive understanding of students will not improve. Outcomes will not improve. Placing a cycle on a worksheet, or a few PowerPoint slides, is only useful where it is mentioned and built into your own modelling, questioning and explanation. This visual cycle – in essence a helpful dual coding tool – is only as helpful as you make it. The main purpose of this strategy is to draw the attention of a student towards the metacognitive cycle, to remind them of the processes that they should be going through and supporting them in making this abstract cycle something that they are explicitly working through each time that they complete a task. Through utilising the cycle on a PowerPoint slide, especially where the part of the cycle you are focusing on is highlighted or made bold, it is useful again to make it explicit to students which part of the process they are currently working through in your modelling. Not only that, but it would help to highlight to students the importance of working through each of the three parts of the cycle, too, rather than just picking and choosing which part they would like to work through, or think is relevant for the task (because we know that students need to be working through all the parts of the cycles to be exceptional metacognitive learners).

Examples

Situation: When delivering a lesson on the formation of a waterfall, I spent time with the class considering how we would be able to write it up into a logical, coherent, well-explained and succinct essay. Whilst doing this, I referred to the plan, monitor, evaluate cycle that I had placed on each slide. The part of the cycle that I was currently working through was also in bold, to emphasise to students which area we were focusing on at that point. Through making explicit reference to the cycle in this format, with the added benefit of the graphic within the slides, I made sure to take time to consider each of the distinct parts of the cycle, and developed student understanding as to why we must go through each of those stages to be successful in our essay writing.

Summary

- Place graphics of the two different metacognitive cycles on worksheets, presentations and so forth as regularly as possible.
- Continue to refer to these graphics as frequently as possible.

Planning documents

What

Fed up with students failing to approach a task in a logical manner? Are students continuing to fail to evaluate their work effectively? Or are students going off on tangents and failing to complete a task effectively? Maybe students are not aware of their strengths or weakness and gaps in knowledge? These are all circumstances that we have come across in the classroom, most likely on a daily basis. In order to combat this, we can provide students with planning documents, which are broken down into the three parts of the metacognitive cycles. Students must then work through each section of this document before they can move on to another task or to complete a further question.

When/How

These planning documents often work best where there is a focus on a student's knowledge of self, knowledge of task and/or knowledge of strategies. Where students are approaching a task where they will really need to consider a wide range of their own knowledge (for example: dates, timescales, formulas), a complex task requirement (with multiple facets to cover and consider) and/or a task where a range of strategies could be used, this template is perfect, and could be used in most, or all, situations on a very consistent basis. In each of these scenarios – where a range of prior knowledge is required, a complex task needs breaking down or a range of strategies is available to students to complete the task – students are likely to struggle. These are common pitfalls that we would plan for and place scaffolds in place for. Perhaps we would use knowledge organisers to plug gaps in knowledge, provide a step-by-step breakdown for task competition and guide students towards one particular strategy? Either way, these types of tasks are incredibly difficult for students to access, and hence the use of the planning document would be extremely beneficial in scaffolding successful task completing.

Why

As soon as you present a task to students where they are required to draw on prior knowledge, or they have a complex task to decode, or even too many strategies (or maybe a weakness in using alternative strategies for a task), some, many or all students are going to struggle. This is not necessarily a bad thing, though. Recalling prior knowledge – i.e. assessing for learning – is one of the hardest things for a student, and forcing that recall will help with long-term memory of the information. Decoding a task, often seen as higher-order thinking, is something that we would often guide students through and model our own thinking and decoding practices. Finally, where multiple strategies are available, students will often not have the confidence to use an alternative, or do not have the recall for an alternative strategy that may be more successful. In each of these scenarios, students will be challenged, but a potential for high-quality learning is opened. In each of these scenarios, students are going to require some sort of scaffold to guide them through the process successfully. This is why the planning documents, such as the one shown below, are so helpful. Through providing students with a document that guides them through each of these difficult areas, we are providing students with the scaffold that they need in order to be successful. It is also possible to provide students with additional scaffolding within the main planning grid, through the use of pointers and key questions. You can adapt questions and pointers as required – for the student or task – in order to make them more relevant. Again, over time, these scaffolds would be removed as students head towards autonomy using these metacognitive processes.

Examples

Situation 1: Having taught students the mathematical content required for their GCSE course, I was noticing how students continued to struggle accessing and completing problem-solving questions. Therefore, I utilised the knowledge of a planning grid. I provided students with laminated copies, a whiteboard pen and a bank of 6-mark problem-solving questions. Students took their time – some working independently, whilst some were in pairs and small groups – to discuss and note down the mathematical knowledge required for each question, the specific requirements of each problem task, as well as the alternative mathematical strategies, and their relative utility for the task. Students began to take these processes on board, and over several weeks utilising the documents became increasingly more successful in their problem solving.

Situation 2: Working with a Year 9 PE group, it was noticeable that students were confused about how to perform the open task of 'design your own high-impact body workout'. Without the structure and guidance typically given to students, they did not have a clear avenue to work on and were very unproductive. To rectify matters, I showed students the processes document, shown below. Students began to make notes based on the different categories, allowing them to consider where their knowledge strengths were, exactly what they needed to do in the task and how they could go about it. Now I always ensure that I have one of these process grids to hand whenever we have a more open task, to ensure that students have the scaffolds that they require to be successful in this type of task.

Summary

- Provide students with tables titled with the three parts of either metacognitive cycle.
- These documents provide students with the opportunity to formally record their thinking for a task, and will help to cement student understanding of these different metacognitive areas.

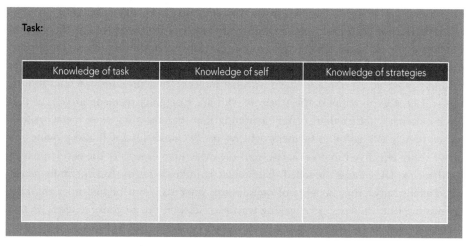

Task:

Knowledge of task	Knowledge of self	Knowledge of strategies

Figure 3.1   An example of the 'Knowledge of' grid that is so helpful in supporting students' understanding of the metacognitive processes

Questioning

What

As it says in the name, the strategy focusses on utilising questioning as a way to embed the metacognitive processes into your lessons. Rather than just asking students content-based questions, you would also ask your students questions around the plan, monitor and evaluate cycle and the knowledge of self, knowledge of task and knowledge of strategies cycles.

When/How

To ensure that students understand the metacognitive cycles, you would need to ask them questions in regard to these cycles on a regular basis. Rather than deciding on a lesson, or topic, that would best suit these types of questions, try to choose some questions that work for you and your classes, and build them into most, if not all, lessons that you teach. The ordering can be left up to you, as well. You may wish to bring in these metacognitive questions alongside content, or once you have finished discussing the content. Over time, you will probably find that they fit seamlessly within the content and strategy-based questions that you are already asking, and don't need to be an 'add-on'.

Why

As with anything, questioning will allow us to assess student understanding. If you are questioning students about the type of planning that they are doing, or the way they will monitor, or later evaluate their work, you are going to be able to build up an accurate reflection of both their understanding of these key words, as well as the ways in which they would approach the tasks more generally when they are doing them independently. It has also been mentioned that metacognition is not something that would naturally move across domains, even within a subject. Therefore, through questioning, you will be able to support the students who are struggling metacognitively in that specific domain, rather than merely assuming that 'because they were metacognitive before, they're still going to be metacognitive now'. Questioning will also provide you with a really effective way to evaluate your own teaching, especially the ways in which you have explained and modelled these metacognitive cycles to students more generally. Equally, any other benefits of questioning students, from higher-order thinking to ensuring that students are engaging with your lessons, are all going to apply to this strategy as well.

Examples

Types of question that you might ask to students include:

- Which planning strategy are you going to use for this task/problem?
- What methods can you use to monitor your progress?
- How are you going to evaluate your final work/answer?
- How did you plan/monitor/evaluate this task last time?
- How are you going to use your evaluation from the last task to support your planning for this task?
- When monitoring, how will you know that you are on track?
- What is your knowledge of self like for this task?
- What range of strategies do you have available to you?
- What is the task requiring you to do?
- What is the same and what varies between this task and the one done yesterday/last week/last month?

The emphasis with each of these questions is either the explicit use of the terms mentioned within the metacognitive cycles, or alternatively drawing strongly on the ideas developed by the cycles, such as evaluating one's own content knowledge on the task.

Summary

- Consistently question students in reference to the different parts of the metacognitive cycles.
- Challenge students on which part of the cycle students are thinking about, and why they are considering that particular area; for example, 'Why do you need to consider knowledge of self?'

Summary

- Metacognitive processes – plan, monitor, evaluate; knowledge of self, task, strategies – need to be explicitly mentioned and utilised within lessons in order to get students to routinely go through these stages when they are working.
- As teachers, we are constantly going through these cycles – in fact, we are metacognitive cycle experts – so we are in a great position to share our thinking with students.
- If students go through these stages on a consistent basis, they will be far more successful and improved independent learners.

Further Reading

Below are some readings exploring these strategies and more from alternative perspectives:

Eggleton, S. (2021). 'Creating a Metacognitive Classroom', Oxford University Press, available at: https://educationblog.oup.com/secondary/english/creating-a-metacognitive-classroom (accessed 4 May 2022)

InnerDrive (2022). 'Plan, Do, Review: The Planning Part of the Metacognitive Process', InnerDrive, available at: https://blog.innerdrive.co.uk/plan-do-review-part-1 (accessed 04 May 2022)

InnerDrive (2022). 'Plan, Do, Review: The Doing Part of the Metacognitive Process', InnerDrive, available at: https://blog.innerdrive.co.uk/plan-do-review-part-2 (accessed 4 May 2022)

InnerDrive (2022). 'Plan, Do, Review: The Reviewing Part of the Metacognitive Process, InnerDrive, available at: https://blog.innerdrive.co.uk/plan-do-review-part-3 (accessed 4 May 2022)

Strickey, T. (2021). 'Metacognition', Teach with Mrs T, available at: www.teachwithmrst.com/post/metacognition (accessed 4 May 2022)

4

Modelling

Learning Objectives

In this chapter we will:

- Review the importance of modelling in our day-to-day teaching
- Develop a range of strategies than can be used to improve your modelling and to support students' metacognitive development.

Introduction

We all know how important modelling is. As the old saying goes, the only guaranteed things in a teacher's life are death, taxes and modelling. Regardless of your pedagogical views, there is unlikely to be a lesson go by where you are not modelling something to students – whether that be a new concept, the introduction of a strategy, the layout of a question or how to break down an exam question, amongst many others. Therefore, with modelling being such a consistent and frequent part of lessons across subjects and key stages, it provides an opportunity to tweak a small part of our day-to-day practice in order to make a significant positive outcome on students.

Within this second chapter crammed full of metacognitive strategies, we will explore a variety of opportunities that you can take to make your thinking explicit. One problem we often have in teaching is that of 'expert blindness' – where something appears so simple (as we are an expert) that it becomes quite difficult to teach to someone else. Due to our expertise within the subject or subjects we teach, it is very easy to forget that we are experts, and so we do not always make the content that should be explicit, explicit. (This is why people often say those who are less expert in a subject can explain it in a clearer manner, as they are forced to consider all of the steps in their thinking, and cannot just go into 'expert auto-pilot'.) Furthermore, experts often make quick-fire decisions, perhaps over the most appropriate strategy to use when tackling a question or problem, based upon our deeper understanding of the topic or experiences with similar questions or problems in the past. Though our students will then get very high-quality modelling, they are missing out on the explicit sharing of the expert knowledge that we have. This is where metacognitive modelling strategies come in. By arming ourselves with a range of strategies, we can ensure that our expert knowledge – including the decisions we make and why – are shared clearly and concisely with students. Small changes can make significantly positive impacts.

Explicit Justifications
What

This strategy places emphasis on justifying the choices that you are making during your modelling. This might be whilst you are at the board, under a visualiser or talking through a PowerPoint, but the focus is on explaining your own choices. Each time there is more than one path that you could go down, for example where there is more than one appropriate (or even just more than one semi-potential) strategy available, this technique suggests that you would then explain your choice to your students. How you explain that would be up to you, but each 'fork in the path', so to speak, would require a justification from yourself.

When/How

As explained above, each time you decide with your modelling, for example, the key word to focus on, a key date or figure to analyse, or a sentence to write, you would have to take the time to explain this decision to your students. One alarm bell should be ringing here – we could take very many decisions during just one short model to students. It would be impossible to discuss them all, without either running out of time or boring our students. Therefore, it would be appropriate to consider whether you have already made this justification to students explicit recently, or if this decision was actually now common knowledge for students. For example, if students had spent the previous few lessons highlighting key words, dates and figures within case studies, then it would not be appropriate to justify this action during your next modelling of a case study. However, it would be appropriate for you to justify a decision that you have not previously justified, or even to justify a decision that you had previously justified, but was a while ago or had not been understood by students. By considering this, you will ensure that you are being explicit about the most important decisions you are making, without repeating previous justifications or learning that students have made.

Why

Within the introduction to this chapter, it was explored how teachers are experts, and that expert blindness can sometimes lead us to missing out key points in our modelling, such as why we are making the decisions that we do. Therefore, the aim of this strategy is to force you into justifying, where appropriate, the choices that you are making during your modelling with a class. By following this technique, you will be ensuring that you are covering all key choices, do not fall into the traps of expert blindness, and allow a light to be shone on your expert knowledge and experience of a topic for students. You will find that through using this strategy, students will understand the content being covered in far greater depth, whilst they will begin to see the connections between content and strategies within your subject area. This is something often associated with mastery maths, but is actually just the aim of all subjects – to ensure that students have a great depth of understanding, and can grow their schema of knowledge for content and strategies too.

Examples

Following the competition of an experiment during science lessons, students are then required to write up their results. This includes the drawing of any relevant tables and graphs. These are two of the more complicated parts of the write-up that students can struggle with the most, firstly due to students struggling to determine which type of graph they should draw, and secondly the scale that they need to use to ensure an accurate graph. In order to address confusion and misconceptions, I begin by explaining to students which type of graph that I will use, and why I have chosen that graph over others. This allows students to understand why one type of graph is the correct one to use, or in some cases a more helpful graph type to use. Following this, I then take time to show students the scale that I have used for my graph, again taking time to reflect on how I have determined the scale, and why that is a more appropriate scale than any other option.

Summary

- Ensure that whenever you are deciding, explain why you are making this choice to students.
- Make sure that you do not assume that students will understand a choice by letting expert blindness take over.

Explicit Processes
What

The technique of explicit processes places emphasis on explicitly talking through the different parts of metacognitive thinking whilst modelling to students. In the first chapter of strategies in this book, metacognitive processes were explored: plan, monitor, evaluate, and knowledge of self, knowledge of task, knowledge of strategies are intrinsic to metacognitive thinking at any age and within any discipline. Therefore, when you are modelling, consider drawing attention to these metacognitive stages you are working through.

When/How

The easiest way to utilise this strategy is by signposting the different metacognitive process stages whilst you are modelling. For example, you could do this by saying: 'Now that I have read the question, I am going to consider what I think this means. This is my knowledge of task. I am doing this to ensure that the answer I write meets the expectations of the question.' By doing this, you are very clearly signposting the metacognitive process stages to them, and also taking that time to justify what you are doing. In regards to how often you do this, the depth of the discussion you make will probably vary, depending upon how much content you need to cover, students' confidence with the content and the key foci of the lesson. However, the opportunity to explicitly refer to the metacognitive process stage you are working through should never be missed. It is no more than adding on one sentence to your spiel when modelling, but that sentence provides clarity for students on what stage you are currently working through and why you are working through that stage now. Furthermore, over time, you would not need to explain to students why you were considering, as in the example, knowledge of task, but rather just signpost students to the fact that you were now working through the knowledge of task.

Why

As repeatedly mentioned, for it is such a key point, metacognition is invisible, and so the more light that can be shone on it, the better. Therefore, by taking the time to make these processes so explicit within your teaching, you will begin to highlight them to students. Furthermore, the overall aim when using strategies in regards to metacognitive processes is to make them automatic within students. Therefore, through our constant reminders of these processes through our modelling, they will, mention by mention, become more cemented in students thinking, and gradually become things that students think about when they are completing activities independently.

Examples

Choosing the right example to model and the way you model that example to students is possibly the most important part of the planning process in maths. When modelling an example to a class I invariably use the visualiser. Using a visualiser allows me to face the class to check for active listening. It also means the students get to see exactly how I work through the example in an exercise book, modelling more closely what their written work should look like. When explaining a concept, I consider cognitive load.

Sometimes the model will be done silently (Barton, 2020). Sometimes a level of narration is needed to scaffold the example. I will always ask students to have 'pens down and nothing in hands' so that their full focus is on the model (Lemov, 2015). With this in mind, often the first run-through of a modelled solution will be silent and the narration will then be added afterwards or added to a second example instead. I consider dual coding (Caviglioli, 2019) and will use manipulatives only when they may add value and not when they may cause extra cognitive load. I use colour in my examples. Highlighters and different colour pens support students to make the links between steps and I will label the steps so that when we are engaged in our deliberate practice, I can ask them which step number or I can question them efficiently about a step where a potential misconception has been identified.

The Walkthrus technique of Narrating the Process holds a crucial role in supporting student understanding of a modelled example (Sherrington and Caviglioli, 2020). I will carefully model each step of the process, choosing which misconceptions students commonly make, and I will model making them. I often correct my tier 3 language on the board: 'This shape spins ..., I mean it rotates. I must be careful to use the correct mathematical language because ...' I break down my exercise book into three columns. I have a column for the worked example and then a second column for their turn. The questions they are asked to do are very similar to the worked example. There will be just one small change in the question so that the students can closely follow the process, whilst more expert students can explore links between the two questions. A third column offers the opportunity to write their reflections. The self-explaining effect of Enser and Enser (2020) supports students to deepen their understanding and the process of writing helps to embed the knowledge into long-term memory. I write down my own narrated reflection as I progress through the problem and the class knows that I expect them to do the same. Through the narration there is opportunity to build a Culture of Error and with a strong Culture of Error, Cold Calling will be used to explore the process and then the links. Teach Like a Champion techniques provide the foundations of the subsequent questioning. By using techniques, such as Stretch It, Right Is Right and No Opt out alongside Wait Time and Culture of Error, good-quality data can be collected to make informed decisions about whether a second modelled example is needed or whether we are ready for deliberate practice (Lemov, 2015).

Dave Tushingham

Summary

- Explicitly detail to students when you are working through each part of a metacognitive process.
- Take time to explain to students why you are working through each part of the process, and what you are explicitly doing.
- Focus on why it is crucial to work through each of these stages, and the benefits that this brings.

Strategy Comparison

What

Strategy comparison requires you to review the alternative strategies available to attempt a problem or task in an explicit manner. In practice, this means rather than just choosing a strategy that we know will work best because of our expertise and experience, we instead take time to model multiple different methods to students, and consider the strengths and weaknesses of each in turn. This could be done in a number of ways, including modelling one strategy and then repeating the same activity with an alternative strategy, or by modelling the two or more strategies side by side on a whiteboard or presentation. Again, you could model through one strategy first and then the others, or you could model through step one for each strategy, step two for each strategy and so forth, allowing you to compare directly what is happening at each stage of a strategy (and not just overall).

When/How

This is typically a strategy that will be used when students have mastered the content a little more. It would be unwise to spend considerable time evaluating the utility of multiple strategies if students were still struggling to comprehend the content that these strategies drew upon. Therefore, this strategy is often used for revision, or to add greater depth to student understanding towards the end of a topic. It may also not be appropriate to use this strategy where there are no real alternative strategies. It would not be worth the time spent evaluating multiple strategies if the alternatives were not at least commonly used. As it is a strategy that will be used more infrequently, greater time can be spent on it during a lesson to ensure the desired impacts of this modelling are achieved. The 'how' of this strategy has been developed above, but to take this further it is worth considering whether you are wanting to explore the actual mechanics of the strategy – that is, the steps taken to complete a task using each strategy – or the strengths and weaknesses of each strategy, and the utility of them (i.e. when they should and should not be used). You may also find that these two rationales actually bleed into each other, which is fine, so long as you have covered the explicit points that you wanted to make with students.

Why

The ability to choose a strategy wisely is an extremely powerful strength of a successful student. We all have students who just 'know' how to go about tackling problems every single time. However, very few students will develop this type of knowledge without explicit input or practicing the same type of questions over and over again with a variety of strategies, so this is where the justification of this strategy comes in. The aim therefore, of this strategy, is to develop students' knowledge of the strategies available to them, their mechanics, and their strengths and weaknesses, better allowing students to choose the most suitable strategies when they encounter problems when working independently. One significant bonus of this strategy is that you are able to synthesise your years of strategy usage and problem competition for students, saving them the time of effort of completing hours' worth of questions.

Examples

During PE lessons, I take time to demonstrate to students the alternative shots or actions that they could have taken. For example, in a football match, I will at times pause the game, and replay the previous move, with the same player, to consider what alternative options they could have taken. For example, if the ball was passed to this player, should they have taken a touch like they did, and then passed it? Or, as I would then ask them to demonstrate, should the player have passed the ball first time without taking a touch? A second option is that the player should not have passed the ball at all, and instead should have began a dribble up the pitch in order to open up more passing options.

The same technique could be used in a range of different spots, from tennis (for example, alternative shots to the same return from your opponent), to cricket (for example, different trigger movements for the wicketkeeper to consider the movements that the batter is making).

Though this is different from the usual modelling of alternative strategies on the board, it allows students to slow down what they are doing, and consider the alternative shots/passes/movements, and so on that they could have taken, and the different outcomes that this could have led to (both positive and negative). Without taking this time out, students just continue playing without actually reflecting on key points within a game. Where students do this, they are not making as much progress as they do when they pause and consider their best options.

Summary

- Model multiple (suitable) strategies to tackle a problem or task to students.
- This can be done one after the other, side-by-side or even step-by-step.
- Begin a discussion with students on the strengths, weaknesses and utility of each strategy, so that students become more flexible in their strategy use.

Visualiser
What

In a world just emerging from a global pandemic, the use of a visualiser no longer seems so niche. With months of live or pre-recorded online lessons, we have all become experts in providing the most 'in-class' experience to students at home. However, as we 'return to normal' the visualiser is not something that needs to be put away on a shelf to collect dust. Rather, it can be a useful tool available to support your modelling on a daily and weekly basis. Rather than talking through a PowerPoint or attempting to model on a board, instead, take your modelling under the camera. There are significant metacognitive benefits of doing this, so long as you provide commentary to the modelling that you are doing.

When/How

When using the visualiser, you would need to decide on the type of metacognitive thinking that you will be commentating on. Though there are numerous things that you could draw attention to under the camera, one interesting thing to draw attention to is the layout of your work. Through modelling with a visualiser, you would be able to provide a commentary over, for example, why you are laying the work out in such a way, why you are starting a new paragraph or a new line of working. You may wish to exploit this strategy just before students get into significant independent work, thus ensuring that students understand what their work ought to look like, and *why*, before they begin their task. Depending on your classroom set-up, the use of a visualiser may be more or less time consuming, which in turn may impact on how likely you are to utilise this strategy. However, ensure that you do create a time within your week to utilise this strategy, even if it is a little effort to set it all up. It is also worth setting up the visualiser so that you can see the class, which is more beneficial for providing a commentary to the class than having your back to them would be.

Why

Though we may model a significant amount on the board, and talk through high-quality PowerPoints, students would rarely see what our 'book work' or 'exam answer' would look like. Yet this is the work that students do all of the time – students are not writing on whiteboards and producing PowerPoints full of their work. Once more, as experts in our fields, we are aware of what the layout to an answer should be, as well as why. I know as a maths teacher, I am consistently explaining the need to show a method, even where students 'know' the answer. What if, for example, the answer is incorrect, and the student does not get any method marks for the build-up to their answer? Through using the visualiser, I am not only able to show the method that I am putting down, but also the justifications for it, allowing me to evidence the 'if I think it, write it', or 'if you type it, write it', phrases that are so commonly used within my classroom.

Examples

I frequently use my visualiser to model to my students how I would tackle GCSE and A-level examination questions, gradually removing the scaffolding before letting them attempt questions by themselves. When I'm doing this I'll always prepare myself ahead of time so I know what the question is going to ask! That's not to say I'll teach to the mark-scheme, but I want to make sure I have at least covered the mark-scheme points.

Take this AQA A-level Biology question for instance:

> Scientists investigated the effect of drinking tea and coffee on reducing the risk of developing one type of brain cancer. The investigation involved 410,000 volunteers and was conducted in ten European countries over a period of 8.5 years.
>
> (a)   From age, suggest two factors that the scientists should have considered when selecting volunteers for this trial.
>
> (b)   Give two features of the design of this investigation that would ensure the reliability of the results obtained.
>
> (AQA A-Level Biology Paper, January 2012, Specification 2410, Unit 2: The Variety of Living Organisms)

If this was the first time I had shown them a question of this sort, I would place a copy under the visualiser and have a pen and highlighter ready and then walk them though how I would tackle this question for myself, speaking aloud every thought process I have. A 'script' might go as follows, placing a stronger emphasis on the words in *italics* as I read them aloud.

> 'Scientists investigated the effect of drinking tea and coffee on reducing the risk of developing *one type* of *brain* cancer.'

> 'I wonder what they mean by 'drinking tea and coffee'? What kind of quantities are they thinking about? Does the milk and sugar matter? What links tea and coffee – caffeine?'

> 'Also, "one type of brain cancer" implies there are lots of types of brain cancer. I need to make sure that whatever conclusions they come up with at the end of their investigation aren't generalised to all types of cancer. I'm thinking this is going to involve a stats test – Spearman's Rank because they're looking at a correlation.'

> 'The investigation involved four hundred and ten *thousand* volunteers. Wow, that's a good sample size. That makes it much more likely that those volunteers are representative of the whole population. The investigation was conducted in 10 *European* countries over a period of 8.5 years. Hmm … Only European countries? Are these volunteers going to be representative of the global population? 8.5 years sounds like a decent time scale to me, but is it long enough to see whether people develop cancer I wonder?'

> 'I wonder how they're going to measure tea and coffee intake because they can't do this as a lab experiment – they can't keep thousands of humans locked up in a lab for 8.5 years! They're going to have to rely on food intake diaries or something like that. That's going to be a bit unreliable – I can't even remember how much coffee I've drank this morning so far …'

Whilst doing this I'll usually use my highlighter to highlight the words I emphasised and jot down key words about my thoughts around the edge of the question stem. With a question like this I'll often scribble a little smiley face or sad face next to points because I know if it's an evaluate question it's going to need a balance of positive and negative points about the experimental design. When using the highlighter I will say aloud, 'I'm highlighting this number 410,000 to remind me about the large sample size'. In other questions with longer stems I'll explicitly state why I am highlighting (or often more importantly *not* highlighting sections).

I'll then leave students to tackle the questions underneath the stem, then we'll mark the answers together and tackle a similar question. This second time I'll remove some scaffolding so I will still read out the question but might say something like, 'Ten European countries over a period of 8.5 years. What do we think about that?' to invite some discussion. Then we'll do a third similar question together but this time I'll remove the scaffolding completely at the start but then invite them to tell me about their own thought processes. I really find this technique slows students down and makes them think about the question more – it reins in those students who like to ignore the question stem and just jump straight to the answers.

Jane Masters

Summary

- Complete your usual modelling, but this time under the visualiser, on paper/ books/exam question, as students would be doing.
- Make sure your model is exactly as you wish students would write up their answers.
- Explain to students why you are making the choices you are with layout; for example, new lines for new workings, new paragraphs, titles and so forth.

What Could the Question Be?

What

One amazing skill that teachers have is the ability to know what a question might be from the answer or method shown. This is due to our thorough understanding of the content of our subject, as well as the links between topics. However, this skill is very rarely shown by students – I know that often I may only challenge students to develop their own questions, as opposed to considering what the question is given a method or an answer. This strategy therefore focusses on providing students with an answer or method and then talking through what a potential question may be considering this information. This would be your opportunity again to draw links from the content and providing your own ideas, illuminating your expertise.

When/How

This strategy is another that you would most likely use once students have mastered the content of the topic that you are teaching them. Once more, if the majority of students had yet to master the main teaching points in the topic, they would probably be lost by trying to work back from an answer to a potential question. However, having said this, there may actually be occasions – where with your topic and your students – it may be beneficial to students' understanding to actually show them the answers and see how they can work backwards.

Either way, this is a strategy that you will use infrequently, typically only towards the end of a topic or for revision purposes. When utilising this strategy, you would need to consider the question that you are working back towards. If your answer or method is fairly open ended, it may be that there are too many alternative questions that could have been asked to get the same answer. This may be exactly what you want, but if you want only one potential question, you will need to think carefully about the method and answer that you are giving to students, ensuring that they could have only come from one specific question.

Why

The main purpose of this strategy is to deepen student understanding of the topic that you are covering. Through modelling how to work backwards from an answer to a question, students will hopefully begin to understand key criteria in an answer, and how this links explicitly to the question that is being asked. This will hopefully help improve the quality and depth of student answers when they are working 'forwards' once again, as they are clear on exactly what factors must be addressed from a question, and exactly how they should be included within an answer. Though this may not seem metacognitive, it is for two reasons. Firstly, you as a teacher are able to share your own thinking, such as, 'Because this key word is referred to within the answer, I know it must be referred to in the question. This shows that we need to use key words from questions within our answers.' Secondly, students will begin to understand key factors that they are looking for, and link this in with the strategies that they are choosing and their approach when completing the tasks themselves independently or within a group.

Examples

Towards the end of each Geography topic, students are required to tackle exam and/or case study questions relating to the learning just completed. The aim of this is to ensure that students are confident (and capable) of completing the most complex tasks in relation to this new learning. However, to further improve student understanding, I take time to consider the questions that could be generated from exemplar answers.

So, instead of giving students these questions (or as many of these questions) as I normally would, I instead draw up a quick answer to one of the exam questions myself.

I provide this answer to students, and then begin to work through it line by line, drawing out key pieces of information that provide a suggestion as to what the original question was. The purpose here is so that students can see how key points in the questions are continuously drawn upon to make a high-quality answer.

Summary

- Begin with a question and draw out key features of it.
- Explain to students how you can use this information to determine the question that could, or would, have been asked.
- Emphasise to students the importance of referring back to key criteria of a question within a written-up answer.

Model Scaffold Use

What

As the idea of differentiating learning outcomes for students gradually disappears, the role of scaffolding – to ensure that all students are meeting a common learning aim – increases. We all want students to be learning the same things, and to push themselves as far forward as possible, but sometimes this is not possible within support. In most scenarios, this is where some form of scaffold is used. If a student struggles with spellings, then provide them with a dictionary. If a student struggles to recall key dates, then provide them with a knowledge organiser. If a student struggles with calculations, then provide them with a calculator. In each of these situations, a student will be provided with a scaffold, and then, hopefully, they will use it, and outcomes will improve. This metacognitive strategy, however, suggests that at the point of providing a student with a scaffold, they should be educated as to what its purpose is, and why it works, before they actually utilise the scaffold to support them in their work.

When/How

This is the type of strategy that can just be built into every single interaction that involves providing students with a scaffold. Of course, if you have already been through this strategy for a student, then you would only repeat it if you provided them with a new scaffold, otherwise there would be no point. You may wish to draft key lines that you use for each different scaffold, or you may just develop phrases over time. For example, 'I am going to provide you with a dictionary, to ensure that you can get more spellings correct. This will allow you to pick up more of the SPaG marks than you currently are.' Here, the student understands the issue (too many incorrect spellings), how the scaffold works (to find the correct spelling) and why this is important (in order to get more spelling, punctuation and grammar (SPaG) marks and push up the student's overall mark).

Why

The benefit of a great scaffold is that it can be quickly provided to students without much need for additional support or guidance, and suddenly the student has got an 'in' to be able to complete the work. With a class of 30 to work with, the quicker we can get scaffolds out to students so that that they can make good progress, the better. Though this is true, it is also true that scaffolds are (or should be) temporary. Therefore, the issue that the scaffold is masking must be addressed in order for that scaffold to be removed. If a student is not aware of the issue that they are having, and why they need the scaffold, and in particular what the scaffold is supporting them in doing, then they are not going to be able to address this gap. By spending time explaining to a student what the purpose of the scaffold is, how it works and the gap it is filling for them, students can be explicitly aware (as opposed to ignorant) of the area that they need to work on. Hopefully, by being made aware of what they need to work on, students can focus on this, ready for the removal of the scaffold. Even if they do not manage to close this gap themselves, a student is certainly not going to make the progress required, unless by coincidence, if they are not aware of the gap or difficulty in understanding is that they already have.

Examples

During an English lesson, there are a variety of easily accessible scaffolds that can be provided to students. The two most common scaffolds are a dictionary and a thesaurus. Typically, students do not have access to either of these resources without their being a need, otherwise students just become too reliant upon them, which is of course not the aim of a scaffold. Students are provided with either (or both) of these resources when I, or a TA, determines they are required in order to support student competition of the task.

However, students are informed why they are being given one of these resources before they can begin using them. This includes explaining what the dictionary or thesaurus is used for, how it works and why it will help students to complete the task more successfully. Overall, this helps students to understand that there are some key words that they are still not quite there with spelling, and there are some words that they use too commonly. Through ensuring that students have spent a lesson using the correct spelling of the word, they are therefore more likely to be correct in their spellings moving forward. Additionally, students will have increased their vocabulary through the use of the thesaurus, and so will be better prepared for their future lessons.

Summary

- Continue to provide scaffolds to students as usual, but take time to explain to a student why they are being provided with the scaffold. What is the purpose of the scaffold? How does it work? How does it help?

- Ensure that students are clear on the area of improvement that they have, and how the scaffold is something temporary that, with time, needs to be removed, like real-life scaffolds on a building.

Summary

- Make sure that you are shining a light on your expertise and experience, and do not let expert blindness take over.
- Take every opportunity to justify your thinking, which provides students with an insight to how your expert brain is working.
- Ensure that you are taking time to model multiple different strategies, and the strengths and weaknesses of these, to make your learners more flexible in task completion.

Further Reading

For further details on these strategies and more, check out these links:

Burns, N. (2021). 'Metacognitive Modelling – Where Does It Fit in the Classroom?', Oxford University Press, available at: https://educationblog.oup.com/secondary/science/metacognitive-modelling-where-does-it-fit-in-the-classroom (accessed 4 May 2022)

Burns, N. (2021). 'Metacognition: 7 Strategies to Use in Any Class', *Tes*, available at: www.tes.com/magazine/archived/metacognition-7-strategies-use-any-class (accessed 4 May 2022)

Ellis, A. K., Denton, D. W. and Bond, J. B. (2014). 'An Analysis of Research on Metacognitive Teaching Strategies', *Social and Behavioral Sciences*, 116, pp. 4015–4024.

InnerDrive (2022). '6 Ways to Improve How You Talk to Yourself', InnerDrive, available at: https://blog.innerdrive.co.uk/6-ways-to-improve-how-you-talk-to-yourself (accessed 4 May 2022)

Kingsbridge Research School (2019). 'Metacognition and Modelling', Kingsbridge Research School, available at: https://researchschool.org.uk/kingsbridge/news/metacognition-and-modelling (accessed 4 May 2022)

Mountstevens, E. (2022). 'Modelling and Metacognition in a Secondary Classroom', Chartered College, available at: https://my.chartered.college/early-career-hub/modelling-and-metacognition-in-a-secondary-classroom/ (accessed 4 May 2022)

5
Questioning

Learning Objectives

In this chapter we will:

- Explore how our main tool for assessment – questioning – can be adapted and tweaked to support the development of metacognitive questioning within class
- Consider some of the ready-to-go resources you could have at all times within your classroom to support instant metacognitive questioning.

Introduction

Teaching is, of course, built around the premise of explaining to an individual how and why we do something, but successful teaching depends on us being able to assess that the individual now does know how and why we do that thing. Assessment is our method, and questioning probably the most used and most practical strategy in our arsenal. Without significant changes to your teaching, a few tweaks to the way that you ask questions can make a significant difference to the metacognitive thinking that is occurring within your classroom.

Within this chapter, there are only five different strategies to explore. Two are very quick amendments to the foci of your questions, whereas the other three require a little more preparation. Each strategy though will need considerable thought applied to it. That is not because the strategies are complex, but rather because questioning is so significant in our classroom. We have a very limited opportunity to ascertain whether students do, or do not, understand what we have just taught them. Therefore, we need to make sure that every question we ask hits the mark. Think of questions as bullets, and they're in limited supply. Each of these bullets (our metaphorical questions) needs to hit the target for us to be successful. So, we ought to take our time and consider carefully where we are aiming. The exact same is true of your questioning. Whether you are an early careers teacher (ECT) or an experienced teacher, it would probably be well worth your time scripting out your questions when utilising these strategies below. Why? As an ECT, you are less likely to have the knowledge of high-quality questions developed from years of teaching, nor do you want to put yourself on the spot and misfire when you're spinning multiple other plates. As a more experienced teacher, it is possible to fall into habits. Habits are not bad either – for most, they will be formed from the refinement of many years' teaching reflections. However, because it is so easy to slip back into these habits, it would be wise to script, so you can ensure you are questioning metacognitively, and not just reverting back to the alternative, high-quality questions that you would usually ask.

Comprehension, Connection, Strategies, Evaluation

What

The idea of comprehension, connection, strategy and evaluation questions comes from the work of Mevarech, which has inspired most of my metacognitive think-ing over the previous few years, and many of the strategies within this book. Within their work, Mevarech and co. highlight the benefit of the comprehension, connection, strategies and evaluation thinking process. The stages of this process are broken down as detailed below:

Comprehension – to develop a clear understanding of the requirements of the task or problem that students have been given, including key command words and the requirements within an answer, such as units or key dates.

Connection – to understand where students have come across a problem or task like this before, and begin to understand the differences, but also the similarities between these tasks. This allows for an evaluation of what went well, and what did not go so well previously, as well as any other learning points from the previous activity that can be carried forward to the new activity. Furthermore, it allows for a consideration of the approaches and strategies used last time, thus providing students with a starting point for the newly given task.

Strategies – the focus here is on understanding the different approaches that can be used to complete the new task presented. As you can see, this leads very nicely on from connection, where a consideration of strategies used for similar activities will have occurred. Within this part, students need to not only be thinking about the alternative strategies available to them, but the relative utility of each of these strategies, their strengths, weaknesses and adaptability. This consideration will allow for the most suitable strategy to be chosen for the given task.

Evaluation – a stage that can never be forgotten. Here, students will consider the successes that they have just had with the given task or problem, as well as the difficulties that they may have had. It is also worth considering here the strengths and weaknesses of the strategy that was used, as this evaluation will lead into the connection stage when students next face a similar problem.

With a clear understanding of these four stages, this metacognitive questioning strategy suggests that questions directed at students should be in relation to these four stages. Students should be explicitly guided through these four parts of task completion (where the first three occur prior to the task, and the last occurs post-task), and questioned suitably. Examples of questions that you could ask are given below in the examples section of this strategy.

When/How

I believe that high-quality teaching would see these questions utilised in every single lesson. Though there may be the very odd occasion where we have a lesson without modelling, I cannot imagine a lesson where questioning does not occur (even if as so limited as to clarify with students that they 'understand' what the task that they have been given requires them to do). Therefore, these questions can be used lesson in, lesson out. It will take time (and evaluation) to ensure that you are referring to the four different parts, but as we know with the metacognitive processes, the more explicitly aware students are of these four different parts of thinking when they are completing tasks, the better. As outlined in the introduction to the chapter, scripting questions, as well as the points that you are going to ask them, would certainly be wise.

Why

The learning benefits shown by the work of Mevarech are significant, as discussed earlier. As a starting point, this is enough rationale to carry out this strategy. However, it is also worth considering our typical student. There will be times where students fail to comprehend a task sufficiently, or where they do not think back to when they have completed similar tasks. There will also be times where students do not pause to consider the strategies available to them, and numerous times where students do not pause to reflect on the work that they have just completed. Therefore, through ensuring that we question students on these areas, we will be helping to drill into them the four different things that they need to be considering when completing a task. Furthermore, we as experts will be going through these four different stages, even subconsciously, every time that we complete a task. Therefore, it is only right that we make this thinking explicit, and try to get students doing it, too.

Examples

Below is a list of different questions that you may wish to ask students, broken down into the four different parts of task competition. There are numerous other questions that you may wish to ask, of course, but this provides you with a starting point. You may also wish to think how you can take these questions from being quite abstract to more concrete, perhaps by bringing in key learning points and your curriculum into the questions.

Comprehension

- What are the key words in the question? How do you know?
- What must be included within my answer? How do you know?
- If I have been provided with a table or graph, why may this be significant?
- Why have I been provided with an image?
- How does the number of marks available for this question link to the structure of answer that I need to provide?

Connection

- When have you seen a question or task like this before?
- What did you do well on when we had the similar task? Why did it go well?
- What did you struggle with when we had a similar task? Why do you think you struggled?
- What support may you need to be more successful this time around? Why will that help?
- What strategies did you use last time, and how well did they work? How do you know?

Strategies

- What are the strategies available to us?
- When would we usually use strategy x?
- What are the strengths and weaknesses of this strategy?
- Will this strategy always work, or is there a safer option?
- Did you consider how effective that strategy was last time that you used it?

Evaluation

- How successful were you in that task? How do you know?
- What went well in that task? How do you know?
- Where might you need greater support next time, and how will that help?
- What will you do differently next time?
- What will you do the same next time?

Summary

- Ensure that you are clear on the four stages of comprehension, connection, strategies and evaluation.
- Challenge students with questions referring to each of these four areas.
- Continue to make it explicit which of the four areas that you are working with, and encourage students to work through these four areas independently when completing tasks, too.

Metacognitive Processes

What

All throughout this book, there is constant reference back to metacognitive process. You can see the value that I hold in them, but also the ease at which they can be brought into many different facets of our teaching. Once again, the more that students are exposed to these metacognitive processes, the more likely they will be to explicitly go through these steps when completing work independently.

So, when questioning around metacognitive processes, the aim is to make these stages as explicit as possible. Again, question examples will be provided at the end of this strategy. The focus will not just be on asking students what stage they are doing ('I'm now considering knowledge of self'), but also why they are doing it, and the actual nitty-gritty of what they are doing (so, I am considering my knowledge of self, which includes me jotting down my key dates and the events, so that I can check I have got the full chronology, before trying to write up my answer). As ever, the 'why' question is your best friend here. Students need to know what they are doing, but to be truly metacognitive practitioners (and conscious of their metacognition), they need to understand why they are doing what they are doing, too.

When/How

This is another of those strategies that can be used within your day-to-day teaching without massive changes. Once you have got into the habit of focusing on those different metacognitive processes and the questions that tie into them, you will find that you're asking these high-quality metacognitive questions lesson in, lesson out. Again, do not be afraid to do this, as learning requires repetition. Our novice metacognitive learners need to learn and re-learn these different metacognitive processes so that they, themselves, are explicitly thinking about them when completing a task.

Why

Short and sweet – the more we refer to metacognitive processes, the more familiar students will be with them, and the more frequently and more confidently students will consider these factors when working independently. We know that explicit consideration of these metacognitive processes will improve student outcomes, and so the more time we can spend questioning students about these processes, the better.

Examples

As with the previous strategy, here are some examples of questions that you could use in class to support your questioning around metacognitive processes. Once again, add your own spin, and bring your curriculum and topics into how you ask these questions.

Plan

- What strategies are you going to use to plan your response? Why are you going to use that strategy?
- What are the key criteria of the task you have been given? How do you know?
- Do you need any additional support before completing the task? How will that help you?

Monitor

- How will you know that you are moving in a positive direction?
- How are you going to keep yourself within the time limit?
- What are the warning signs that you might be looking out for?

Evaluate

- How will you know that you have met the task success criteria?
- How are you going to improve next time?
- What support might you need to be more successful next time, and how will this help?

Knowledge of self

- What content do you know about this area?
- How do you know that content is relevant?
- What gaps do you have in your understanding? How are you going to address those gaps?

Knowledge of task

- What is the task asking of you? How do you know?
- What are the key criteria for you to include?
- Have you seen a task like this previously, and if so, how did you tackle that task (were you successful, unsuccessful, how, why and so on)

Knowledge of strategies

- How could you go about approaching this task?
- How confident are you with each strategy?
- Which strategy is probably most suitable for this task? How do you know?

Further examples

I have used metacognitive questions and positive narration with my Key Stage 3 history students. When reviewing a piece of work in progress or assessing learning, I use questions such as, 'If you were not sure of the answer, what did you do to answer this question?' – providing students with a strategy or building a student's toolkit of what to do if they get stuck or cannot recall the information. Likewise, using positive narration, I then delve deeper with, 'Why do you think that strategy would work for student X?' 'Is there a question where you could have used that strategy?' This then opens the opportunity for further modelling by me or peers on utilising such strategies, such as graphic organisers, reframing the questions or reviewing other responses – making the thought behind the learning process explicit. Students can be defeatist; however, this process provides them with a thought process before they give up, increasing opportunity for success. I have found that using this positive narration equips them with a learning toolkit that runs parallel with the historical knowledge they are developing.

Metacognitive questions do not just feature at the review stage of a piece of learning or sequence of lessons. I try to use them in the preparation and monitoring stages too, asking students to reflect: 'Where have you completed an activity/task/question like this before, and what made it a success?' Likewise: 'What is the purpose of the task at hand?' 'What does the examiner want?' 'What preparation do we need to do to tackle this activity head on?' Sharing this train of thought with students and making it an explicit part of the learning process helps develop them as active learners. Promoting the use of these skills independently in the future. I like to build on peer learning through metacognitive questioning too, using peer assessment mid-task to provide dialogue between learners: 'How are you keeping yourself on task or to the point?' 'Is there any area you are finding difficult?' 'What strategy have you used/will you use to overcome this?' – training our young people to be self-reflective learners through peer and teacher dialogue.

I am a firm believer in planning questions for my lessons, content questions, challenging and metacognitive questions. Planning these helps ensure they are delivered with purpose and that I can plan for misconceptions. The natural growth of a lesson means additional questions often appear but having a foundation of questions in your bank, ready to use, helps keep the metacognition element explicit as opposed to an afterthought. The planning of these questions does not need to be onerous; they can be jotted down in a planner or Post-it to help guide. The more I have planned and the more I use metacognitive questioning and positive narration, the easier and more natural it becomes in my teaching. This is the same for the peer metacognition dialogue: the more students get used to questioning one another in this way, the more embedded it becomes in their own practice. To support this process, peer assessment verbal sentence starters or question starters have enabled productive student conversations.

Sarah Falcon

Summary

- Continue to make the metacognitive processes explicit within your teaching by using them as questioning points.
- Question students regarding the stage that they are working through, and why they are working through it.

- Utilise the questions provided above to force deep thinking from students around the different parts of the metacognitive cycles.

Questioning Cards

What

Questioning cards require a little more preparation than many of these other activities, but once sorted can be used every single lesson without any further preparation. In fact, to save you some time, there are pre-made questioning cards (which you will find out more about as you read on) available to all of you who are reading this book.

Questioning cards provide a gateway between you, as the teacher, asking students questions, and then moving towards peer-to-peer questioning and groups questioning each other. The aim of the questioning card is to give students physical (laminated) cards containing a key question, which revolves around the ideas of plan, monitor and evaluate (that good old metacognitive cycle once more). These cards can also be supplemented with sentence starters on the reverse, providing that graduated scaffold for students who need them. You may ask students these questions to begin with, and then as they become more confident in answering, you may move to pair or group questioning.

When/How

This activity will often be utilised where you have longer to spend questioning students (or getting them to question each other). There are two main reasons here. Firstly, it takes a while to distribute a resource to students, especially packs of questioning cards to different pairs or groups. Secondly, because these questioning cards consider the main three processes – that of plan, monitor and evaluate – there is a considerable amount for students to think about, and also discuss. You would not want to do this in a small space of time. Equally, you are not going to do this for every small activity (here, you leading with a few well-planned and well-targeted questions would be suitable). Instead, you will probably use these cards when considering a more significant task, perhaps a lengthy exam question or a small project. To use these cards successfully, I would recommend handing them out to students and you asking the questions for the first few times you use the cards. This will allow students to develop a level of familiarity with the cards and questions, and also practise using the sentence starters where appropriate. Over time, you will be able to graduate to pairs and group questioning, a strategy explored in the next chapter in slightly greater depth.

Why

For successful metacognitive practitioners, these questions that you will be asking are second nature. They will be asking themselves these questions all the time. Once again, the focus of this strategy is on making these questions automatic for students, and ensuring that they are being given the most exposure possible to these crucial points as possible.

Another key point to note is the benefit that these cards can have for many students from a working memory perspective. Questioning students can be overloading, and there will be many occasions where students know the answer, but have been unable to stay focussed on the depth and length of the questions that you have been asking. Getting students to focus on one card at a time helps to remove that issue. Furthermore, the sentence starters will hopefully take away the 'ers' and the 'oohs' from the classroom, as students have a way to begin to formulate their answers.

Have you provided working/evidence/ units etc.?	Does it fit the format asked for by the question?	Does the solution make sense?
My solution makes sense because ________. My solution doesn't make sense because ________.	I know my answer fits the format asked for because ________.	I have provided evidence/ units/examples. I know I had to include this because ________.

Figure 5.1 Examples of some of the questioning cards that could be used in lessons, including both questions that could be asked and sentence starters to support improved student responses

Examples

With my Year 11 Religious Studies class, student comprehension of exam questions is crucial in order to ensure success in their GCSE exams. In order to support students with the development of the comprehension, all students in the class have been provided with the comprehension questioning cards. All students are expected to have these in each lesson, and can use them to question each other, as well as self-question when they are given tasks.

This Year 11 group do not have the sentence starters on the reverse of the cards, as they are sufficiently familiar with these questions and their responses that they are not required. However, students still carry and utilise these cards to ensure that they are overly familiar with the key points of comprehension. This overfamiliarity ensures that under the pressure of mock and real exams students can recall these questions from their long-term memory. This helps to ensure better student outcomes overall.

Summary

- Questioning cards are pre-produced resources that you can print off and laminate so that you are always ready.
- Provide students with a pack of cards so that they have the questions you are asking in front of them.
- Encourage students to utilise the sentence starters, which you can have on the reverse of these cards, to support higher-quality and deeper answers.
- Train students to use these cards so that they can begin to question each other, increasing participation ratio.

Questioning Matrix

What

The questioning matrix is a superb idea from Jon Haines. Though these questioning matrices were not initially put together for metacognitive purposes, they do provide high-quality questioning opportunities, as well as some metacognitive benefit. The best way to understand the questioning matrix is through taking a look at the example below.

QUESTION MATRIX	IS? DOES? PRESENT	HAS? DID? WAS? PAST	CAN? POSSIBLITY	SHOULD? OPINION	WOULD? COULD? PROBABILITY	WILL? PREDICTION	MIGHT? IMAGINATION
WHAT? EVENT							
WHERE? PLACE							
WHICH? CHOICE							
WHO? PERSON							
WHY? REASON							
HOW? MEANING							

Ask better questions...

Figure 5.2 A template for the questioning matrix, demonstrating the type of questions which can be generated for high-quality sources

The key to a high-quality matrix is through the diagram or image chosen in the centre of the matrix. A poorly chosen source of information will not allow for questioning to occur from the matrix, or even if questioning could occur they may not be high-quality questions (and so they become wasted). Therefore, it is hugely important that when using this strategy you do take the time to choose an appropriate source.

When/How

This is a strategy that you will use more infrequently, as you will need to spend a lengthier amount of time on this activity to make it worth it. Furthermore, not only will you need to script some questions, you will also need to design the matrix and have it printed for students. Do not ask too much of yourself and start trying to do this every lesson. Furthermore, it is also worth considering whether the content you are trying to use the matrix with is important. Do not set yourself a target of using the grid once a week, as if the content is not suitable you'll end up with a less than useful source, and hence a lot of wasted questioning (and time).

As with the other strategies, it would probably be worth noting key questions from the matrix that you would like to ask students. Before asking students, it would also be sensible to give them an allotted thinking time to consider the source before you start questioning them on it. You will also find that, over time, students will hopefully 'see' what the good questions are (as you will have been modelling them previously), and may start to ask each other. This is where this strategy can go from you leading to a more discussion-based group task, which is explored in the discussion chapter coming later.

Why

The questioning matrix provides an opportunity to ask some wonderfully in-depth and poignant questions, so long as the appropriate source has been chosen. Assuming that it has, there is also the benefit of showing students how you develop such high-quality questions from the source. If students can understand your thinking in terms of the insight you have when preparing questions, this will hopefully allow them to improve their questioning (and critical analysis) of sources, too. This will also shine a light on the range of questions that can be asked for students. It should mean that when students believe that they 'know' a topic, they now understand that they could be asked many different questions from many different perspectives, and to truly 'know' the content they need to be able to answer all of them.

Examples

Within history lessons, the questioning matrix is the cornerstone of most lessons – it is the consistent resource that would be seen each time that you walked into the room. The reason for this is that it provides such a rich source of thinking lesson in, lesson out.

It is important to acknowledge that resources are easier to find for History than most other subjects, as much of our work is around source analysis. Therefore, it is not that time consuming to put together hugely helpful resources, allowing this strategy to be used on such a frequent basis.

As this strategy is used on a more frequent basis, students have become familiar with the type of questioning that they know will be coming. This means that students understand the depth of the thinking that they need to undertake during their personal thinking time, before I begin my own questioning of students. Again, as students are so familiar with these questions, it has led to two different benefits. The first is that students are now more able to ask each other these same insightful questions, thus increasing participation ratio. Secondly, as students are frequently exposed to high-quality questions, slightly outside of the norm, they are better able to adapt to alternative questions and exam questions than they were previously. Students are more capable of answering a variety of questions, and demonstrate a greater depth of understanding than they did previously.

Summary

- Download the questioning matrix template as demonstrated above.
- Find suitable sources that would be interpreted by students to place in the centre of the matrix.
- Provide students with thinking time before questioning them using the matrix.
- Train students to use the matrix so that it can become a paired or group activity, thus increasing participation ratio.

Compare Strategies, Plans and Answers
What

One area of metacognition that I place such high value on is students' knowledge of the strengths, weaknesses and utility of different strategies of approach for tasks. This may be from the way that they approach the planning to a task, to the mechanics of how they complete it, right up to the way that they produce their answer and the alternative ways that this can be done.

This strategy places a focus on questioning students about the alternative options they have. Much like in the modelling chapter, where time would be spent literally showing students the different ways that they could plan, complete or write up a task, this strategy revolves around questioning students about these different options. Though I should not really favour one part of the metacognitive processes over the others, I really do believe that the more fluency that students have over strategy (including the ability to use a range of strategies, and knowing when to, and not to, use each strategy) the better a student they will be, and the more likely they will be to deeply understand content in the future.

Much like some of the strategies above, focus your questioning on the alternative strategies. What are the strengths and weaknesses of both? Why would you use one strategy over another? When does that strategy work well, and when does it not? Many of these questions have been covered above, but some other examples are provided at the end of this strategy.

When/How

Naturally, this type of questioning cannot really come before students have mastered the content that you are teaching them, and have had a range of strategies modelled to them. Furthermore, before students are questioning the strengths and weaknesses (and so forth) of these different approaches, it would be wise to spend time discussing them first. This could be done in the lesson before you know you are going to be questioning students in this way, or within groups, where your input is limited (so that you are not just spoon-feeding students the answers).

Therefore, this is not the sort of questioning line that you will take up each lesson, or even every other lesson. It will be required once students have got a very strong understanding of the content, and a developing confidence with alternative strategies available to them.

Why

For a learner to have mastered a topic, they need to understand it inside out, forwards and backwards, left to right. Students need to be able to complete tasks in a range of different contexts, and be adaptable above all else. In order to be this type of learner, a student *must* have an extremely clear understanding of the strategies that they have open to them, and when they should, or should not, be using them. A student may know one strategy inside out, but as soon as the contexts of problems start changing, as soon as the format is mixed up, as soon as the values used get changed up, that student will often start to struggle. Therefore, by consistently questioning students about the strengths, weaknesses and utility of a range of different strategies, we are forcing them to open their eyes not just to the content, but the mechanics of these tasks, and to really take time to consider the best approach that they can take to complete the task. If we value anything above all else, it really needs to be students' abilities to work flexibly with a range of strategies and approaches.

Examples

As with the examples above, the example here will focus on a range of different questions that you could use within your lessons to support with questioning around strategies. These questions will be broken down into strategies, planning and answers, so that you can see how questions can subtly change depending on the type of comparison and evaluation you are doing.

Strategies

- What strategies could we use? How do we know we can use them?
- What key information do we have which suggests a certain use of a strategy?

- When would we typically use each of the different strategies?
- Is one strategy safer than another?
- Is it better to use the strategy that you are more confident with, but is less suitable for this problem, or the strategy that is more suitable, but you are less confident with?
- Have you used the strategy discussed for this problem before? How did it work? Any reflections?

Planning

- What are the different ways we could go about planning?
- Are there any formal planning requirements for this task?
- How long do we have to plan? Does this impact on the planning strategy that we could use?
- Does the information that we have available to us limit the strategies we can use to plan?
- What is the aim of the planning, and therefore which strategy may work best?

Answer

- What are the alternative answer layouts?
- What are the strengths/weaknesses of each?
- Does the question dictate a specific type of layout?
- What will be the easiest way to demonstrate your thinking and answer to a marker?
- What would be the clearest way to lay out your answer?
- How would the different layout methods be understood by a complete novice? Would they understand each/either of the methods equally, or does one make greater/less sense to a novice than the other?

Summary

- Directly question students about the potential strategies, planning model or answer layouts that they could use.
- Drill in on the strengths, weaknesses and utility of each different method.
- Develop student understanding that not all strategies work as well on all occasions.

Summary

- Questioning is a key part of each and every lesson that we teach. With it being such a commonplace (and significant) strategy, it provides a perfect area that we can tweak ever so slightly to lead to significant metacognitive benefits for our students.

- Ensure that your questioning revolves around points of metacognition, including the metacognitive processes, comprehension, connections, strategies and evaluation, and alternative approaches and their respective strengths, weaknesses and utility, rather than subject specific knowledge or content.
- You will need to ensure that students remain clear on the subject knowledge, so that they can focus in directly on the metacognitive thinking that you are wanting them to focus on.

Further Reading

For further readings on general approaches to metacognitive questioning, the following may be of interest:

Cambridge University Press (2022). '20 Metacognitive Questions to Ask in Primary Science Lessons', Cambridge University Press, available at: www.cambridge.org/gb/education/blog/wp-content/uploads/2021/08/20-metacognitive-questions-to-ask-in-primary-science-lessons.pdf (accessed 4 May 2022)

Classteaching (2021). 'Why Is This a Metacognitive Question', Class Teaching – Find the Bright Spots', available at: https://classteaching.wordpress.com/2021/11/10/why-is-this-a-metacognitive-question/ (accessed 4 May 2022)

Hester, R. (2021). '20 Metacognitive Questions to Engage Your Science Learners', Brighter Thinking Blog, available at: www.cambridge.org/it/education/blog/2021/08/04/20-metacognitive-questions-to-engage-your-science-learners/ (accessed 4 May 2022)

InnerDrive (2022). '9 Questions to Improve Metacognition', InnerDrive, available at: https://blog.innerdrive.co.uk/9-questions-to-improve-metacognition (accessed 4 May 2022)

Laurie, A. (2022). 'How to Develop Learners' Metacognition Skills with Effective Questioning', Maths No Problem, available at: https://mathsnoproblem.com/blog/teaching-practice/how-to-develop-learners-metacognition-with-effective-questioning/ (accessed 4 May 2022)

6
Discussion – Ready to Roll

Learning Objectives

In this chapter we will:

- Consider the conditions required for successful pair and group work
- Identify the benefits of having successful pair and group work
- Evaluate a range of strategies to support metacognitive discussion and learning within your classroom that require limited preparation and experience.

Introduction

Discussion is one of those teaching techniques that always sounds nice, but never quite seems to deliver the desired results – whether that be due to student behaviour, getting groups wrong, or students lacking the subject knowledge to have an in-depth and beneficial discussion.

Therefore, before we even consider the range of metacognitive strategies based around discussion, it is wise to consider what helps to make a discussion activity all the more successful.

1   Ensuring that your groupings are correct. You will probably already have students in a seating plan, but this does not necessarily mean that students are going to be already sitting with the best people to have a discussion with. You know the behaviour of your students best, so move students around as required, for example to ensure that students who may go off task are not in groups together.
2   Mixed-ability groups may appeal, but this may not always be best, either. The theory behind this idea is that the most able student will lead the discussion, and their ideas will slowly seep into the rest of the students in the group, supporting their learning. Though this can often work, it may also be worth considering whether this just leads students in a group just to rely on that 'higher attaining' other, rather than getting stuck in themselves. Maybe it would be best to group similar ability students together so that they can take the conversation to a deeper level than they may otherwise be able to go in a mixed-ability group. If you want mixed-ability groups, ensure that expectations are clear that there can be no 'hangers-on', and that all group members must be contributing.

3   Provide students with extremely clear expectations. This is possibly the easiest way to deal with any potentially undesirable behaviour popping up. Where you have made expectations to students very clear, it will allow you to follow through with any relevant consequences. Where there is a lack of clarity over expectations, students are adept at finding the loopholes! Furthermore, by having very clear expectations, including over outcomes, students are clear on what they need to be achieving during their task. So often, students will go off on tangents, or just forget the overall aim of the task. Where objectives are clear, students will be far more able to stay on task and deliver the outcomes that you desire for the activity.

4   Provide students with scaffolding. We know in day-to-day learning that students require suitable forms of scaffolding, and nothing changes when we get students to work within groups. This scaffolding could potentially take two forms – one around task expectations, i.e. support on what a good answer looks like, what good notes look like, and so forth; and the other looks at content support. For a standard independent task, students would receive a scaffold with both the content and task requirements (whether that is an alternative explanation, TA support, knowledge organisers or a different method), in order to ensure that they meet the desired outcomes of the task. We cannot just rely on students within a group to provide this scaffold for each other, and so it is crucial to consider what support students may still require in order to be successful in the activity/task that you have just given them.

There are of course numerous other considerations when planning discussions and group work – far too numerous to go into further detail about here. However, the links at the end of this chapter provide you with further reading if this is an area that you would like to consider in greater depth.

So, once discussion has been established within the classroom, why would you be considering metacognitive discussion? As highlighted in previous chapters, we can best support student metacognitive development through making our own metacognition explicit – whether that be through modelling, processes, questioning or another form. However, we also need to provide students with the opportunities to be able to reflect and discuss their own metacognitive thinking on a more regular basis than the odd occasion that a student is cold-called on in class. Discussion activities provide students with the opportunity to explore and delve into their metacognitive thinking in a comfortable, pressure-free environment. Not only does it provide students with a greater opportunity to discuss their metacognitive thinking, it also provides them with the opportunity to start to make metacognitive discussions the norm. We as teachers will consistently be discussing areas that went well, how other areas can improve and so forth. In fact, this is often the main premise of a weekly staff CPD session or faculty meeting. Therefore, if we, as educational professionals, understand the benefit of these types of discussions – so much so that we have incorporated them in our standard teaching week – why, therefore, would we not want these conversations to become commonplace for students?

Therefore, considering the power of metacognitive discussion, it is time to review some of the different strategies that you can use to build this feature into your lessons. However, these strategies are split across two chapters. The strategies that you find within this first discussion chapter require limited preparation and are more straightforward to put into practice. The discussion strategies found within the next chapter may require greater preparation and/or more experience of developing metacognitive discussion. This way, you will be able to choose the correct strategies to be effective in your introduction of metacognitive discussion with your classes.

Questioning Cards
What

Questioning cards, as shown below, are a range of cards that provide students with key questions that they can ask each other. Additionally, these cards have potential sentence starters on the reverse, providing students with a scaffold if they are struggling to frame their response to the question. These cards or key questions could be projected onto a whiteboard, printed out for students or even laminated so that they could be re-used over and over again, helping to cement them as a regular part of your classroom practice, as opposed to a one-off activity.

When/How

These questioning cards are the perfect scaffold for when groups are just getting the hang of their metacognitive discussions. To begin with, all students and all classes (ages and abilities) are going to need this sort of scaffold. You may decide that for some classes, they don't need the sentence starter, though it is the sort of scaffold which really should not harm. Over time, you may decide that students no longer need the sentence starter, or maybe there are some questions that students have now got into their repertoire for discussions so that you can remove them from the questioning card pack. Equally, you may decide that there are certain areas that you want students to focus on, and therefore you just provide them with those questions for the discussions that they are having. As mentioned, you could print off and laminate these questioning cards, thus allowing you to have a resource that you can bring out at any time to support students. They become the sort of handy resource that you always have with you, ready to support a metacognitive conversation whenever it springs into life.

To facilitate discussion, students can question more than one student in their group. From this, students can begin to see the similarities and differences in their answers, thus leading to a conversation about how, and why, these have arisen. It may be that you need to give students some linking questions, such as why and so what, in order to push the conversation along, rather than just a group of students asking each other independent questions.

Why

Students really struggle with direction and objectives in a discussion activity, and this is often even more challenging in a metacognitively framed discussion, where subject content can appear subtler, and the expectations can be vaguer. Therefore, to keep students on task, these cards provide the clear guidance that students need in order to support their metacognitive discussions. Furthermore, by providing students with the sentence starters, students are all able to have a go at answering the question; it is just the depth of their answer that will vary. However, through introducing build-on questions, such as why and so what, students will be forced to go further in their thinking and justification, helping them to explore their metacognitive thinking more deeply. Finally, and always a good bonus, this strategy is such a simple one to introduce at any point. Through having a set of laminated questioning cards available, any opportunity for a group discussion can be taken without having to go on a massive tangent, or with the requirement to do extensive amounts of planning.

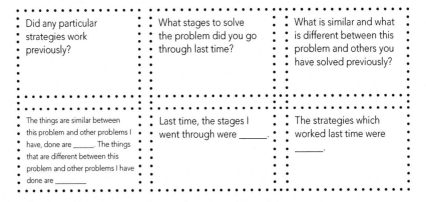

Figure 6.1 Examples of some of the questioning cards that could be used in lessons, this time focusing on connections, including both questions that could be asked and sentence starters to support improved student responses

Examples

During Business Studies A-level lessons, it is crucial that students take the time to consider how new case studies and questions relate to previously analysed and attempted questions. Students often approach case studies and questions from fresh, rather than considering where they may have attempted a task previously, and how their reflections on that task would lead to better outcomes in the current task or question.

Students are familiar with these questions due to my consistent use of them during questioning of the students. However, as students are now more familiar with these questions, as well as the requirements to consider the connections between case studies and questions, they are now in a position to question each other. This occurs after students have had time to personally review the case study, and make their own notes and reflections around 'connections'. Then, in much like a 'think, pair, share' type approach, students begin to question each other, ensuring that students are all forced to consider the different connections involved with the task. Once students have taken the time to question each other, they will then approach the task, and have far improved outcomes than had they not gone through their connections thinking.

Summary

- Provide students with a set of questioning cards around the topic area/metacognitive area that you are focusing on.
- Provide students with sentence starters on the reverse of the cards to ensure that students are all able to access and explore the questions.
- Suggest linking questions, such as why, and so what, to students, to turn questioning into a full-on discussion.

Questioning Matrix

What

The questioning matrix provides students with a visual source within the centre of the page. Around this, students are given a range of question starters, allowing them to develop questions and ideas around the source that they have been given. Through this, students can begin to draw up questions for each other, which in turn will allow them to build up a conversation, as they explore alternative interpretations – and the reasons for this – of the source that they have been provided with. The source that you provide within the centre of the matrix can also be changed for the group (i.e. scaffolded suitably), and can work for all subjects. It is also a naturally differentiated activity, which allows students to explore in as much depth as they are academically able to.

When/How

The questioning matrix is certainly a strategy that would need to be planned, unlike the questioning cards strategy which could be drawn on in a second's notice. With this method, particular time, care and attention will need to be spent on choosing the correct source to provide to students. It is crucial to decide on the areas that you want to direct students towards, rather than just choosing an exciting source for the matrix, which may actually not bring about the type of discussion that you are desiring.

Due to the consideration over the source that you are using, it may be that this is a strategy that is used more infrequently, perhaps at the start of each topic (as a judgement of what students are already aware of), or towards the end (as a judgement of what students have learned), or even both. This is certainly not the type of resource that is going to be used in every single lesson! Furthermore, despite the fact that it can be relevant to every subject and all levels within that subject too, there are of course some subjects that this strategy lends itself to more (e.g. history), than others possibly (e.g. mathematics). However, just because it is hard to find a suitable source does not mean that this strategy is not worth exploring.

Why

The joy of this strategy is that students really can explore it in as much depth as they are able to. Small groups are able to take their conversations to a greater depth than they may be able to in a more structured strategy, such as the questioning cards. Furthermore, there is a vast array of interpretations to each source that you provide to students. Not only will this generate a huge amount of high-quality academic discussion, as well as a significant insight for yourself as to the knowledge students have, but also a hugely beneficial opportunity for you to explore students' differences in thinking with them. There really is no limit to the amount of metacognitive exploration that can be done here.

QUESTION MATRIX	IS? DOES? PRESENT	HAS? DID? WAS? PAST	CAN? POSSIBILITY	SHOULD? OPINION	WOULD? COULD? PROBABILITY	WILL? PREDICTION	MIGHT? IMAGINATION
WHAT? EVENT							
WHERE? PLACE							
WHICH? CHOICE							
WHO? PERSON							
WHY? REASON							
HOW? MEANING							

Ask better questions...

Figure 6.2 A template for the questioning matrix, demonstrating the type of questions that can be generated for high-quality sources

Examples

In my maths lessons, the questioning matrix is used to highlight poorly produced graphs and tables, often from real-world scenarios. Students need to consider the question starters around the outside of the matrix in order to analyse the 'poor-quality' source within the centre of the matrix. The benefit of this strategy is two-fold. Firstly, more students are being forced to consider the weaknesses of the given source. Previously when I completed this activity, I would only be cold calling on a handful of students. However, with this strategy, all students are being forced to think and answer these questions within their groups. Secondly, the matrix provides students with some key questions they can be thinking about. Previously, again where I cold-called students to provide weaknesses of the given graph or table, I had not provided students with any key points to consider, and so sometimes students were limited or confused in how they could answer. The matrix provides a level of scaffold and familiarity, so students are able to question each other, and are aware of the type of thinking that needs to be occurring within their group.

Summary

- Questioning matrices include a key source that has been selected following consideration of learning aims.
- Students build questions from the matrix, and begin to explore alternative interpretations, and the reasons for these.
- Build on students' alternative interpretations to understand their metacognitive thinking – why have they chosen certain questions, why have they approached answers in different ways, where has their context of interpretations arisen from?

Quiz, Quiz, Trade

What

In quiz, quiz, trade, students are all provided with a card containing one question. In this activity, students are required to find another partner and ask them the question. The second individual will then ask the first individual their question. When both students have answered their questions, they swap cards, and then go off in order to find a new individual, who they will repeat the process with. Over time, this may mean that students end up missing some questions/repeating the same question, but when this begins to happen on a frequent basis, it becomes a natural point in which to end the activity.

In regards to the content of these cards, they can be metacognitively focussed, of course. Therefore, rather than questions exploring the content of a topic, students will have questions around strategies that they used, strategy utility and effectiveness, weaknesses in approach, gaps in student knowledge, and so forth. Linking back with metacognitive processes, it may even be that these quiz, quiz, trade cards follow along one of the two metacognitive processes: plan, monitor, evaluation, or knowledge of task, strategies and self. *Two birds, one stone.* It also may be that if you have the questioning cards handy these are the ones that you use for this activity. Not only does this avoid additional planning, but it also ensures that students are continually considering the same questions, just in a greater amount of depth.

When/How

This activity is again one that you may need to be considering in your planning, rather than introducing it with a click of your fingers within a lesson. Within this scenario, it will be crucial to ensure that all questions provided to students are relevant to the task or content that they have just been covering, and that students are clear on the quality of answers that they are expecting. However, the type of questions that this strategy will be focusing on, such as 'Why did you choose that strategy?' and 'What are the strengths and weaknesses of that strategy?', are the types of questions that students need to be familiar with, and so utilising the same questions, and this activity, on a more regular basis would help to ensure that that is occurring. The examples below are sure to provide you with ideas on when, how and how often you should introduce this activity.

Why

Quiz, quiz, trade provides the opportunity to liven things up for students a little. Of course, successful learning does not just occur because an activity is different or fun, but where students are still engaged in the same high-quality discussions (led by your high-quality and thoughtfully put together question cards), then it certainly cannot harm that students are having more fun and are more engaged. This task can also be adapted to challenge students to answer every single question – though be careful that students do not just start to offer half-formed answers in haste to swap cards and move on.

Examples

Quiz, quiz, trade is a strategy that I use for student evaluation once they have completed an assessment. Students are given questions around how they prepared for the assessment, their reflections on their actual assessment (such as which strategies did you use that were successful), and then questions around how they will prepare for a future assessment.

These are the questions that students would typically need to answer during an 'exam wrapper' task. By completing the quiz, quiz, trade activity on these types of questions, students are forced to consider all of the factors of an exam wrapper, but they are also forced to both justify their choices to other students, as well as take on board other thoughts and ideas. Though it is absolutely amazing that students go through these evaluation questions independently, there is an added bonus of having to explain it to another student (narration of evaluation ensures that students further consider if it is a reasonable and sufficient reflection), as well as taking on board the evaluation from other students (allowing students to consider further alternative options). Overall, this is a great strategy to support further student participation and evaluation.

Summary

- Provide students with one metacognitive question card each. Get students to pair up, and then ask each other the question that they have got. After answering, students swap cards and find a new partner.
- Consider providing students with sentence starters to ensure a higher success rate in answering the questions.
- Carefully consider the questions that you are providing students. Keep the same language as usual, so that these questions begin to come automatically to students, and do not 'dumb down' questions to make the activity more 'fun'.

Graphic Organisers

What

Graphic organisers – whether that be a bubble map, a double bubble map, tree diagram, Frayer model or so on – is a visual tool used to categorise different information and focus on different areas of thinking. Graphic organisers themselves could not just take up a whole chapter within this book, but actually probably need their own book entirely to understand their utility and importance to student learning. In short, the main types of graphic organisers, and the thinking that they stimulate, are as follows:

Circle map – defining within a context

Bubble map – description in a concise manner

Double-bubble map – compare and contrast

Flow map – sequencing

Multi-flow map – understanding cause and effect

Fishbone diagram – understanding causes in depth

Tree map – classification

Brace map – structure of a whole

Frayer model – detailed research into a concept or topic

Bridge map – identify analogies.

You can see here that the different types of thinking stimulated by each of these graphic organisers means that each type lends itself to a different type of learning situation. If you are wanting students to look in-depth at causes, then the fishbone diagram is the one that you want. If you are wanting students to consider classification, then the tree map is the one. The purpose of this strategy, though, is not just to choose the correct graphic organiser (though of course choosing the correct strategy is crucial), but for the discussion that would come after students complete the graphic organiser themselves.

Once you have chosen a graphic organiser, and students have managed to complete it (individually, pairs or even in groups), students will then come together to compare what they have written down. Have they got the same causes and outcomes? Have they got the same descriptive words, or the same analogies? If they have, or if they have not, this is where a discussion will ensue. Why do students have different ideas? Why have they approached it in different ways? As ever, to support a strong discussion here between students, it would probably be wise to provide students with some key questions or discussion points up on the board to scaffold this task.

Alternatively, you may suggest to students that they must place the information that they have just learnt or been given into a graphic organiser, and not stipulate which organiser to use. Students would then have to consider the purposes of the different organisers, before deciding on which one to use. When they have decided, students can come together to discuss which organiser they have chosen, and the reasons for this (i.e. which strategy have they chosen, and why).

When/How

Building graphic organisers into your teaching routine is possibly one of the hardest things to do. If you do not already use them, or you only use specific types, it can be hard to start using them, or to use alternative types, as they are just so far removed from what you are usually doing in lesson. Therefore, to begin with, you may just wish to focus on two or three different types that you are confident with using, and then bring them into your planning and lessons at appropriate times. This may mean that to begin with, you are only using a graphic organiser once a week or so.

Over time, this is maybe a strategy that you will bring in towards the start of a topic (what do students know before being taught) or at the end (what have students learnt). You may even get students to continue to add to their organiser through the teaching of a unit! However, this is not going to be a strategy that you are using every lesson – and even if you think that you could see a purpose each lesson – a little bit of variety is probably best. Therefore, choose your two or three favourites and most applicable organisers, consider where these fit in with your subjects (content/curriculum wise), and gradually build up the frequency of use as you, and your students, get more confident using them.

Why

Graphic organisers themselves are just a terrific way of categorising information. However, because they provide two choices – over which type of organiser to use, and then the information selected to put into the organiser – they provide the perfect opportunity to spend time discussing choices, and the reasons behind them. It is this choice that brings out students' metacognitive thinking – why they have made the choice, why they favour one organiser over another, why one organiser is better suited to this information than another, and so forth. Where an explicit cognitive choice can be explored, fantastic metacognitive development will be made for students.

Examples

We devised our CPD around metacognitive principles and drilled down on how graphic organisers can be used to support student planning. Equipping students with the skill of selecting and using appropriate graphic organisers successfully has led to greater student outcome. The outcome is demonstrated in written performance but also verbal breakdown of how to approach a task. Two frequently used graphic organisers are the Frayer model and a Venn diagram.

The Frayer model has been used to introduce new terminology. In psychology, students often struggle with the term 'reductionism', therefore we used the Frayer model to explore its definition, how to use it in a sentence, examples and non-examples. This explicit process of 'unpicking' a term created discussion, analysis and deeper processing from the students, supporting student growth and confidence in using reductionism in their essays. This use of a graphic organiser has then grown and is used as one of our retrieval practice templates. Students are provided with a blank Frayer model with a term in the centre. They then must complete the appropriate boxes thinking back to where they have used it, what it means, who the common misconceptions are – creating a multi-purpose Frayer model: learning, metacognition and retrieval.

Venn diagrams are the second graphic organiser that provides a scaffold for students facing the more challenging comparison questions in Psychology. When faced with a comparison on approaches in psychology, students often cite approach X, followed by approach Y, creating almost two separate answers, failing to compare. Using a Venn diagram has enabled students to visualise the components of the approach and draw upon similarities and differences. Combining graphic organisers with modelling adds the additional layer of support for students when first using Venn diagrams (and all graphic organisers). Through this process of successful modelling, in the future when tasked with a comparison question, we use questioning to stimulate student reflection: 'How do we tackle this type of question?' 'How could we organise our thoughts?' – leading students to the response of a Venn diagram and having them model to others their thought process and actions when completing this task. With many graphic organisers, in exam conditions they can be replicated quickly if needed. This is reinforced when delivering whole-class feedback and action points – sharing examples of 'quick Venns' that were scribbled on the notes section of the exam paper to demonstrate good and achievable practice to support success.

Sarah Falcon

Summary

- Either choose an appropriate graphic organiser, or allow students to choose their own, for the organisation of given or learnt information.
- Get students to discuss their choice of organiser (why, benefits, drawbacks), as well as the information that they have included (why they have, why they have not included certain information).

Working Backwards

What

This strategy, much as the name suggests, places a focus on working backwards from a final answer or written answer back to the original task or question. This could be done through providing students with a printed answer or method, and getting students to create *a* or *the* question originally posed. Alternatively, students could be provided with a range of different answers and methods, alongside a range of different original questions and tasks, and are then required to match them up correctly together. To develop this strategy, students will need to be discussing in their pairs or groups about the questions they believe could have generated the answer given, or how they have paired their questions and answers.

When/How

This is a strategy that will work well when students have already demonstrated confidence with the content within a topic that you have taught. Used too soon, this strategy may be too challenging for students, and actually confuse matters over the learning that they are trying to master. However, when students have begun to master this new content, working backwards provides students with the opportunity they need to begin to deepen their understanding of the new topic. What better way to stretch students and to deepen their understanding by getting them to work backwards?

Why

The purpose of this strategy is for students to spend time considering the reason that different strategies may have been employed. Through analysis of different answers and methods, students will be discussing why they might have used those different methods, and how that links in with the type of question that might be answered. Additionally, through conducting this type of discussion task, students are going to be considering the range of different appropriate questions that they may be asked considering their content and strategy knowledge. This will hopefully mean that students are more prepared for a greater range of questions during assessments and examinations than they would have been otherwise. We all know how limited classroom time is, and so we are unable to get students to practise each variant of question for each topic area. Through utilising this strategy, students will be far more aware of the questions they could be asked and the strategies that they can utilise to attempt the question or task.

Examples

Pupils are naturally inquisitive and as well as being great problem solvers they are also great problem setters, so encouraging pupils to set their own problems creates opportunities for metacognition and self-regulated learning. Working backwards is a strategy I utilise as part of whole-class teaching as well as when working with a small group of pupils where the pupils are provided with an answer and they are then challenged to come up with a suitable question/word problem which would result in that answer.

I often use this strategy at the beginning of my maths lesson which I refer to as the 'Discover' aspect of the lesson where I present pupils with an answer in the form of numbers, words or a diagram. Pupils are then challenged to create their own question or word problem allowing them the opportunity to function mathematically. Children work collaboratively engaging in mathematical talk using stem sentences, acquired vocabulary and their understanding of concepts when generating questions. Whilst children are engaged in this activity they are making connections between the maths that they complete from lesson to lesson and the real world.

The working backwards approach promotes deeper thinking and understanding than solving a given problem as children are expected to anticipate what knowledge or procedure will be required. This will often include carefully considering the context of their problem, the size of the numbers that they are going to use, the vocabulary to direct and guide the reader, the operations required and how all of this information needs to be combined to create the question that results in the desired answer.

The application of the strategy working backwards promotes a conjecturing atmosphere where children spend time discussing, drafting, editing and setting questions which can be solved in a variety of ways. During this task some pupils generate very simple calculations using a single operation. Other pupils who are confident and have a greater understanding of maths will confidently suggest contextual word problems which involve a range of operations or several steps with greater computational difficulty.

The working backwards strategy and initiation of own question encourages children to use higher-order thinking skills and retrieval practice by activating prior knowledge to create problems which can focus on a range of concepts, skills or procedures resulting in a variation of questions. Pupils plan, monitor and evaluate the effectiveness of their question and whether they have achieved their intended outcomes. Pupils also enjoyed engaging in peer-generated problems and providing feedback to their peers to help them improve their question setting.

Farhana Patel

Summary

- Working backwards challenges students to consider the question or problem which may have been set, considering the answer or solution that you have provided them with.
- Students need to discuss the alternative strategies utilised in their answers to successfully develop a range of suitable questions that may have been posed.
- Working backwards will deepen students' understanding and challenge their linear thinking of receiving and then answering a question.

Odd One Out

What

The 'odd one out' strategy is another one that is obvious from the name. This strategy involves providing students with a range of options, perhaps a range of questions, answers, opinions or strategies, and getting students to determine which one they believe is the odd one out. Ideally, each of the options provided to students can be argued as the odd one out for different reasons, allowing a more fluid conversation between pairs or groups of students. Where only one option can be argued as the odd one out, discussion can be limited, for as soon as students are confident about which one is the odd one out, there is little left to discuss. Where students have to determine how each of the options is the odd one out, a deeper and more fluent conversation is able to take place.

When/How

The odd-one-out strategy is one that can be used at any point within a lesson or topic. With many of these strategies, students need to have a strong understanding of the subject content so that they are able to start effectively engaging with metacognitive elements. However, odd-one-out tasks are hugely effective at developing students' initial understanding of a topic area, making them the ideal strategy to use at any point.

The greatest point to consider is that highlighted above, where the options all need to be made the possible odd one out. The task can become significantly too limited where only one option is the odd one out. Much like with a multiple-choice question, where the options need to draw upon common misconceptions, as opposed to just random alternative answers, the odd-one-out option also needs to draw upon common ideas, strategies and misconceptions.

Very often, these tasks can be displayed on an interactive board, without the need for any further planning or printing. Students can then discuss the task in their pairs or groups, and students are then able to feedback to the whole class following their smaller group discussion.

Why

The odd-one-out strategy is extremely powerful in cementing student understanding of the initial content of a topic. As well as highlighting correct examples, it is possible to highlight non-examples and common misconceptions. Positively, this task allows students to think deeper than just true or false, or example or non-example, by formulating ideas as to why each of the different options could be the odd one out. Metacognitively, students are being forced to challenge standard approaches to a task, and to challenge in-the-box thinking. Overall, students should become more adept at challenging the most obvious, or conventional, answer.

Examples

The odd-one-out strategy is a useful teaching strategy as a support in the identification of misconceptions and in the development of student schema. Choose three words that are related in some way and one word that is not related. Students must identify the correlation between the three words and why the fourth is the odd one out.

For example, after teaching students about the physical and human causes of uneven development, I wanted to ensure that students could differentiate between these different causes so created an Odd-one-out question. The three correlated key words were: tectonic hazards, natural resources and climate-related diseases; all natural causes of uneven development. The odd one out was colonialism, a human cause of uneven development. Students were expected to identify the correlation between the three natural causes of uneven development and identify that colonialism was a human cause of uneven development. If students are unable to do so, it becomes clear that they have not developed the necessary schema to identify and group these causes of uneven development correctly and that this is something that needs re-visiting.

This strategy can be taken even further by choosing words that are only tentatively correlated. This supports students to develop their schema, connecting topics or words that they haven't previously correlated.

When you're using this strategy, ensure that you provide students with an opportunity to explain why the odd one out is so, to ensure they have the solid reasoning you expect behind their choice.

Molly Scott

Summary

- Provide students with a range of options – potentially questions, answers, opinions, methods, or strategies – and get students to determine which one is the odd one out.
- Challenge students to find a way to rule out each option as the odd one out.

- Supports students' ability to challenge conventional approaches to questions and thinking by not just ruling out the obvious answer, but thinking about it in a deeper and more systematic method.

Think, Pair, Share

What

Think, Pair, Share is a commonly used technique across key stages and subjects. It is already often used for the purpose of improving student answers and increasing dialogue within a classroom, and the metacognitive use does not vary much either. In Think, Pair, Share, a question would be posed to the class. Students would then be given some thinking time, of around 30 seconds and upwards. At this point, students would then turn to their partner (I would always recommend students sat next to each other, rather than forwards/backwards to avoid unnecessary turning around). Students then share their thoughts with each other. At this point, depending on the class, and experience of using this strategy, students could then discuss their respective answers to develop one, superior answer. Once students have had the opportunity to share and discuss, you as the teacher could then take ideas from different pairs of students throughout the class.

When/How

This strategy is a fantastic one to use on a frequent basis. Though it does allow for the generation of discussion between students, it does not need students to move around, nor extremely lengthy periods of discussion, as students are just focusing on one point at a time. Therefore, this is something that you would probably be able to use for most lessons. However, it is worth considering the type of questions you are asking students to consider. Too shallow, and students will not need the thinking time, let alone the discussion time. Too deep, and students will need far too long to complete this quick discussion strategy. Once again, we revert back to the Goldilocks level of being just right. To make this strategy successful, you will need to ensure your pairings are suitable, and so you may need to move students around a little bit. However, if you already have a seating plan, the ability of students sitting next to each other to work together has probably already been considered.

Why

Think, Pair, Share allows you to build in thinking time. This is something that can be lacking, for a variety of different reasons, such as pressure to get through content and behaviour management. Furthermore, Think, Pair, Share provides a nice gateway into metacognitive discussion, as it is still initially led by yourself, before the emphasis is placed on the students. The overall purpose of this strategy, therefore, is to get students to begin to share their ideas, and vocalise their understanding. This is perfect for students who lack a little confidence and do not want to share with the whole class, but who would be happy to speak to the person next to them. This is such a commonly used strategy, you probably have a whole swathe of reasons why you use it.

Examples

Think, Pair, Share is a versatile strategy that can be used at various points in a lesson to help students to plan, monitor and evaluate their own learning. Using Think, Pair. Share can also be a valuable tool to reduce the likelihood of individual students opting out of challenging thinking tasks because they know they might be selected to share at the end. In this way, it is also a supportive set-up for cold-calling, which can sometimes be an uncomfortable experience for some shyer students.

Situation 1: You have just modelled how to answer a key question for the lesson in the target language, for example 'Qu'est-ce que tu fais pour rester en forme?' (What do you do to stay in shape?). You give students one minute of thinking time to formulate their own response to the same question. Be careful not to talk during the thinking time; this can be distracting for students, even if you mean well. After the thinking time, ask the students to practise their answers in pairs. Here, you could also allow students to provide feedback to one another, which may or may not need to be scaffolded, depending on the stage of your learners. Finally, after paired practice, randomly select a handful of students to share their responses. You might also find it valuable to tell all the students (before they share their answers) that you will be asking other students to translate/summarise their peers' answers. Once again, this can avoid students opting out if they think they've avoided being selected to share.

Variations: In the above example, it can be helpful to conduct the Think, Pair, Share as a Write, Pair, Share, asking students to make notes on mini-boards or in their books during the 'think' section of the task. This will allow you to circulate and watch out for any misconceptions, as well as help some students think more explicitly about the task at hand.

For this type of speaking task, if your students have access to a recording device, such as a *talking tin* or a school laptop/tablet, you can ask students to record their answer as part of the 'pair' section of the task. They can practise with their partner first, then record and re-record as necessary. Then during the 'share' section, the student needs to only play back their answer, rather than answer live. This can be particularly beneficial for evaluating their own pronunciation and intonation, which would otherwise not be possible through a live response.

Eliza Wade

Summary

- Challenge students with a question, and provide them with at least 30 seconds' thinking time. Once this time is up, students need to discuss their answer with the person sat next to them.

- For more confident or able groups, these pairs then need to develop a joint (and improved) response to the question.
- Choose pairs or groups to share their answers with the class. This should lead to better thought-through and greater depth of answers.

Partially Worked Examples

What

Partially worked examples are exactly what they say on the tin. In this method, you would provide students with a question and the steps needed to reach a final answer, but with certain parts rubbed out. This could be whole lines of working, or it could be partial lines of working. With this strategy, students would need to consider in groups what is missing, and what they believed needed to fill the gaps. Students would need to come to an agreement in their groups in order to complete the task.

When/How

This task will often be used with students once they have got a firm grasp on the new content you have been teaching them. If students are not even sure how to complete a question moving forwards, then they are extremely unlikely to know what they are doing working backwards! It might be worth completing this task the first time with a question that you have just completed. Therefore, students will understand the mechanics of what they are doing with this strategy. Again, without this, all student brainpower may be used on understanding what they are supposed to be doing, rather than the actual task at hand.

An additional, or alternative, scaffold is to print off all of the different stages/steps that are needed to complete the blanks. This way, students are not required to 'think up' the content, and instead can just stay focussed on the ordering of the stages. However, with more confident groups, or groups that are familiar with this activity, you may want them to be thinking both about the content and the strategy.

Regarding frequency, this is again a task that will probably be used more infrequently, due to the knowledge and confidence that students will need with specific content before they can successfully complete a task like this.

Why

The purpose of this strategy is to ensure that students truly understand the stages that they are going through, and why. It is so easy, with repeat practice, for students to become almost robotic with their work, as they complete stage 1, then stage 2, stage 3 (and so forth) before getting a final answer. By challenging students to work backwards, we are shaking them out of this mindset, and forcing them to consider the stages in greater depth. Which stage comes before that? Why? How do I know? It also makes students consider what they should be seeing at each stage of their answer or solution. This is an invaluable skill due to the monitoring abilities that it develops in students. If a student can understand what an answer ought to look like a third of the way through, halfway through, four-fifths of the way through, and so on, then they will be able to identify where things have gone wrong *before* getting to the end of their answer. This ability to monitor, one of those metacognitive process stages, is crucial in ensuring that students are moving towards a successful outcome, and do not find an answer which is completely irrelevant to the task actually provided.

Examples

'Rather than setting lower expectations for students, they [teachers] support them [students] to reach ambitious goals using a range of scaffolding processes that guide them on the way' (Sherrington and Caviglioli, 2020). Partially worked examples are common practice in my classroom to ensure that all students can reach the top. This can look different depending on the knowledge of the students taught and the question considered.

Novices think differently from experts (Didau, 2019). In my lessons, for novice students, a significant amount of each example that they take part in may already be completed for them. The students practise using the foundational knowledge required to be able to access the problem whilst seeing how these foundational pieces of knowledge support to solve a more complex problem. The resource will often be created from a full worked solution for a mathematical process where key calculations have been blanked out. This scaffold is then faded out through the deliberate practice activity as students understand better the concepts covered, and become more competent in using the processes required for success. In other words, more of the key parts of the solution are blanked out (Pershan, 2021). For more expert students the scaffolding will be less frequent and less substantial, allowing for greater exploration of the process taught.

It may be that the scaffolding looks different. For example, the scaffolding may be in the form of a hinted question where the students are directed to consider a particular piece of knowledge or a particular method when answering the question.

Another approach to scaffolding the work for novice students could be that they are simply expected to engage with the first stage of the process. Let's consider the process of solving simultaneous equations by elimination:

Solve $2x + 3y = 11$ A

$3x + 4y = 16$ B

Step 1: Multiply equation A by 3 and multiply equation B by 2

$6x + 9y = 33$ C

$6x + 8y = 32$ D

Step 2: Subtract equation D from equation C

$Y = 1$

Step 3: Substitute y = 1 into equation A

$2x + 3 \times 1 = 11$

$2x + 3 = 11$

Step 4: Solve for x

$2x = 8$

$x = 4$

I want all students to understand the complete process but this could create extraneous cognitive load for some students. I will therefore ask more novice students to focus on subtracting one equation from the other (step 2), whilst more expert students will go through more of the steps. The students can then be expected to take on more and more of the steps as they progress through the exercise. Expert students may be asked to explore a second approach to solving the equations. Multiplying the first equation by 4 and multiplying the second equation by 3 for step 1 also works, for example (Barton, 2020).

Accessibility through easy-to-use, formatted sheets is important so that students do not experience extraneous cognitive load. These can be straightforward to create by simply adding the model solutions and then using stickers or marker pens to blank out the relevant parts of the solution. Choosing what to blank out relies on an understanding of the misconceptions that students have and, to be successful, the sequencing of the fading out of the process through the deliberate practice key to students understanding the concept. I have learnt errors along the way for the order in which I fade out information in my examples and designing a set of deliberate questions where the solution is gradually faded out has been valuable for the quality of the examples and explanations I offer today.

Dave Tushingham

Summary

- Provide students with an incomplete solution or answer.
- Challenge groups to complete the solution using their knowledge of the strategies associated with that topic area.
- This approach ensures that students become familiar and confident with the mechanics of a strategy, both working forwards and working backwards.

Find Someone Who

What

In this activity, students need to find another student in the class who has done something different from them, which you specify. This could be, for example, a student who used an alternative strategy to that student, or it could be that the students used the same strategy, but one student who would not use the strategy again, whereas the other still would. Ideally, the 'find someone who' would be a difference based upon a metacognitive area, such as strategy use or evaluation. Once students have found someone in line with the criteria you have set, they then need to discuss their differences of opinion, and consider whether this now changes their opinion, or whether they are sticking with their initial thinking.

When/How

This strategy works well after students have been completing tasks but using alternative strategies. For example, once students have learnt how to complete a set of questions in a range of different ways, the 'find someone who' strategy then becomes one that would be extremely appropriate to use. To ensure the smooth running of this activity, you would need to make sure that there are sufficient students using alternative strategies within the class, or sufficient students evaluating their strategy use in an alternative way. Without this, the activity will very quickly fall down if students are unable to 'find someone who'. It would also probably be wise to provide students with a set of sentence starters that help them to explain their choices to the partner once they have found them. As this is quite a complex conversation – with students having to explain their alternative choices or relative differences – students will need some guidance on how to make this a successful conversation. It may also be wise to model this conversation with a teaching assistant or student within the class first, so that students both know what their conversation should be sounding like and are aware of some key lines or phrases that they can use to help structure their explanations.

Why

One of the biggest difficulties with evaluation of any task or question is the inability of students to consider the alternative approaches that they could have taken or the evaluation of the strategy that they themselves used. Although, and as mentioned within this book, there are ways that we can support student evaluation within the lesson, they can all take a large portion of time away from other learning. 'Find someone who' is a strategy that forces students to consider alternative evaluations of their approach, or alternative approaches, without having to repeat the whole task again. Therefore, this strategy allows a quick way for students to verbally explain their strategy choices and quickly understand the alternative approaches.

Examples

I normally use this strategy in my Geography lessons when students have just completed a task involving the comprehension and use of a case study. Due to the different interpretations of the case study, as well as the different weighting that students will put on different facts, figures and pieces of information, students will have lots of differences that allows good levels of discussion.

To support this activity, I will often provide students with key areas that I want them to consider, and 'find someone who'. These areas include:

- Find someone who came to a different conclusion than you did.
- Find someone who used a different write-up strategy.
- Find someone who used alternative personal accounts.
- Find someone who used alternative events to you.

The most important thing for students is not just to find someone who in order to meet each of these criteria, but actually to discuss with students why they made different decisions. It is crucial that students are not trying to prove to each other why they are right or wrong, but instead just to listen to the different choices that other students made, and why they made them. The outcome here is that students are aware of the different approaches that they could have taken, and the justifications for taking these choices, without having to carry out the task multiple times.

Summary

- Task students with finding a student who has used an alternative strategy or has evaluated their strategy use in a different manner (e.g. they would not use the strategy again).
- Get students to talk their partner through the evaluative choices that they have made.
- It would be wise to model this type of conversation to students, as well as providing them with sentence starters or key phrases, to help guide and scaffold high-quality conversations.

Summary

- Discussion is a hugely powerful tool within the classroom. Most beneficially, it improves the student participation ratio, so more students are doing more thinking.
- Take time to consider your group layout and expectations with group work to ensure that it is positive and progressive, rather than just a waste of time for all involved.

- There are more discussion strategies than the other areas of metacognition. Equally, these strategies require more student confidence and understanding than the other three areas too, as they are not led by you.
- Ensure that you have identified the discussion strategy that focusses on the precise area that you are wanting students to improve with.

Further Reading

These further readings provide you with an insight into effective group work. Further readings relating to metacognitive discussion will be provided in the next chapter.

Budden, B. (2022). 'When Should You Use Group Work?', *Tes*, available at: www.tes.com/magazine/teaching-learning/general/teaching-learning-when-should-you-use-group-work (accessed 4 May 2022)

Durrington Research School (2019). 'Using Group Work for Effective Learning', Durrington Research School, available at: https://researchschool.org.uk/durrington/news/using-group-work-for-effective-learning (accessed 4 May 2022)

Howe, C. (2018). 'Tes Focus on … Group Work', *Tes*, available at: www.tes.com/magazine/archived/tes-focus-ongroup-work (accessed 4 May 2022)

Metallurgy and Materials Department (2022). 'Tips for Effective Group Working', University of Birmingham, available at: www.birmingham.ac.uk/schools/metallurgy-materials/about/cases/group-work/tips.aspx (accessed 4 May 2022)

Quigley, A. (2013). 'Top 10 Group Work Strategies, The Confident Teacher, available at: www.theconfidentteacher.com/2013/01/top-ten-group-work-strategies/ (accessed 4 May 2022)

7
Discussion – Yet More Strategies

Learning Objectives

In this chapter we will:

- Evaluate a range of strategies to support metacognitive discussion and learning within your classroom that require greater preparation and experience.

Introduction

This chapter builds from the previous one exploring effective discussion activities within a lesson, as well as a range of easier to implement strategies to support the development of metacognitive discussion in your classroom. However, that is not to say that these strategies are significantly more complex. The strategies within this chapter may require a bit more preparation and/or experience utilising other metacognitive strategies.

This chapter will be laid out in the same format as the other chapters exploring metacognitive strategies, and so you will be able to determine which of these strategies will be the best to introduce within your classroom.

Misconception Discussion
What

Provide students with a question, and a range of alternative answers, each of which contains at least one commonly presented misconception. Give students a set amount of time (linking back to those expectations of group work), in order to identify the misconceptions that have been demonstrated. To challenge students further, and in order to develop their metacognitive thinking, students will then need to discuss the misconceptions that they have found, especially around the areas of:

- How has this misconception come about?
- How could the individual have discovered this misconception earlier?

- Do they need a change in strategy?
- How would you suggest that they amend their approach for this task if they were to do it in future?

To support students with this task, it may be worth putting these questions – or others that you choose and support the activity outcomes – up on the board again, to support and guide a successful discussion between students.

When/How

This is a very low-planning activity – or at least it will be where we are activity planning around common misconceptions demonstrated by students. Very often in lessons that I have seen, a teacher will provide a clearly 'incorrect' answer that demonstrates a misconception, and will build a good narrative from this. In the scenario, there would be very little work (if any) for the teacher in making this a task that students could work on within their groups, while the only change needed possibly is developing more scenarios where a range of different misconceptions are demonstrated.

In regards to frequency of this strategy, it is one that could be delivered every few lessons – or at least as often as you are explicitly addressing misconceptions through your modelling or teacher-led talk. Furthermore, the depth of misconceptions that you provide students, or the number of different tasks in which you are asking them to explore, can be changed, in order to shorten or lengthen the task time as required. It would therefore be possible to give students just one misconception task, and only 5 minutes' discussion time, if you needed to get it done quickly, or a half-dozen alternatives and a whole lesson, if you could spare the time for such a lesson.

Why

The beauty of this strategy is not just the metacognitive benefits that it holds – such as analysing the effectiveness of alternative strategies, considering methods of monitoring and how to make improvements in the future – but also the subject-specific benefits that it has. Misconception analysis is something that high-quality lessons will always consider. Tackling head-on the common issues that students face is the ideal way to prevent students from making them in the first instance. This strategy not only allows you to do that, but also allows you to explore the metacognitive implications as well – another *two birds, one stone* strategy. Furthermore, there is little to no planning time, and the strategy can be amended to fit any time block that you have available within your lesson. This is such a flexible and handy strategy to have in your toolkit.

Examples

Mathematics can be a minefield of both known and unknown student misconceptions for teachers to navigate. Rather than avoid these I tackle them head-on and make them a deliberate part of engaging students' metacognitive thinking. My template for the framing of these questions is 'Mr Woolaston's Mistakes' (the students love it when I make a mistake, so they are always eager to find them!).

I include four prompts to guide students' thinking during this task:

1   What was the error made?
2   How should I have done it?

For both prompts the focus is on metacognitive knowledge. I want students scanning the working-out focussed on identifying the error and considering if they can resolve it. Students are asking themselves 'Do I know this topic well enough to find the error?' and once identified 'Do I know enough about this topic to do this question correctly?'

3   Why do you think I made that mistake?

Here is where the good stuff starts to happen. Students are now developing their metacognitive regulation by observing my error and trying to put themselves in my shoes to see why it was made. They are retracing my thinking through the problem looking for the divergence from the correct and diagnosing *why* I might have made that error. This gets the students thinking deeply and comparing the given solution against their internal schema for that skill.

4   Verdict – Mistake or misconception?

Here, the students have to consider what the difference is between a mistake and a misconception. I want them to be familiar with the language and the distinction so they can reflect on their own errors and self-diagnose.

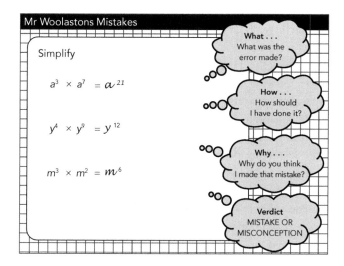

Figure 7.1   An example lesson slide, showing the thinking and discussion prompts

Being exposed to, and deliberately focusing on the analysis of these misconceptions has made my students more careful and accurate in assessing their own thinking. There is less false confidence and overestimation of their ability as they see regularly how easy misconceptions can take root. This activity works well as an individual task but is also very well suited to Think, Pair, Share structure. Prompt 4 in particular is a fantastic catalyst for discussion between students.

Ryan Woolaston

Summary

- Provide students with a completed task or answer which demonstrates one or more common misconceptions that students may demonstrate.
- Get students to highlight the misconception, as well as evaluate key metacognitive points, such as strategy strength, methods of monitoring and changes to future attempts.
- Provide students with as many misconceptions and as much time as you have. This task can be squeezed into 5 minutes or span an 80-minute-plus lesson.

Good, Better, Best Answers
What

I am not sure that a strategy has been considered, amended, pushed and criticised as much as this one. The idea (at least the metacognitive idea), behind this strategy is to present students with around three alternative answers to the same task or question. Each of these answers will be different, with one representing a good response, while another response is slightly better than that and the last response is the best. Students will then consider the three different answers that you have placed in front of them, and decide which answer is the best. However, this is the new, metacognitive version, and so students will not just pick the 'best' answer.

The three answers provided need to be very similar in their levels – and will very often only be separated by around a grade (or at most two) in their quality (where it is possible to 'grade' answers). Equally, all answers may have the same 'grade' given, but specificities within the answers may be different. The purpose of the metacognitive consideration is not just to decide which one is best, but explore why. What are the best features of each answer, and why? What strategies have been used within the different answers, and why? What features appear in each answer, and what is their positive or negative impact? The number of different questions that can be asked here is huge, but in short, students need to be discussing the intricacies of the different answers, the alternative strategies used, any planning or monitoring demonstrated, and evaluating the effectiveness of it all.

As mentioned, providing students with discussion points or key questions to debate and discuss, again displayed on an interactive board, will be crucial to the success of this activity. Without this, students are either going to just label one answer as superior to the other, and explore no further, or simply give up and wait for the 'answer'. Either way, the purpose of the activity will be defeated.

When/How

Answer analysis is not something that can be done in every single lesson. Without a good understanding of subject content, as well as a strong grasp of the alternative strategies and methods that could be used to complete such a task, students are not going to be able to complete this discussion activity in sufficient depth to warrant running the activity. Therefore, this task will only be successful where students have got a solid understanding of both the subject content and the variation of strategy used to plan, monitor, evaluate and complete the task.

Furthermore, where exemplar answers are not frequently available (and, of course, they are often not available for lower grades, for similar grades, or in certain subjects, such as maths), there may be an increase in workload in order to produce these models. However, the positive thing here is that when they are done, they are done. It may also be possible for you to collaboratively plan some of these exemplar answers with colleagues, so that they can be shared out within a faculty or trust, rather than each subject specialist producing (and duplicating) example answers that someone else has already spent hours producing.

Why

The main purpose of this activity is to improve students' evaluation skills. Students need to be able to look at a piece of work – whatever that may be – and evaluate the strengths and weaknesses of it, from a subject perspective, as well as a metacognitive perspective. Students ought to understand when one strategy has worked more effectively than another, and why. Using this strategy, therefore, students should be able to develop their understanding of what makes a good answer, and why, improving their all-around evaluation skills.

Not only do students improve their evaluation skills, however, but they will also massively improve their subject knowledge. This task is of course a variation of a tried and tested strategy that has been used for 'yonks', and so the subject-specific benefits of this strategy for students will remain.

Examples

A technique we have been using within our department is what we call 'Good, Better, Best'. This technique involves choosing a difficult question from an exam and then using the examiner report to craft three responses to that question. The responses ideally are all good but varying levels of good as generally our students are fine at picking out awful responses. We write the answers in by hand down the left side of the document, ask students to rank the three answers and then ask students to write a justification for their choice. The purpose of this is to expose students to common exam questions, the marking practices that lie behind them and the common mistakes made by their peers in the past. Additionally, it provides a model for them when writing their own answers.

Question	Chlorine reacts with sodium and with hydrogen. Compare the structure and bonding in sodium chloride and hydrogen chloride.

Read the three answers below and rank them 1,2,3.

1 being highest and 3 being lowest, use the criteria at the bottom and your own knowledge to inform your decision. Write your answer in the boxes on the right.

Justification

(Total 6 marks)

Justification

(Total 6 marks)

Justification

(Total 6 marks)

Figure 7.2 An example of how students must record their justifications for their answers

After students have completed their justifications, they attempt a similar question, hopefully implementing their newly gained understanding and crafting a better response than they otherwise would have done.

Ryan Badham

Summary

- Provide students with around three completed answers, which vary little, or not at all, in terms of a grade that they may be given.
- Provide students with suggested questions and points, such as 'why is answer one the best', or 'consider which approach to this question was most appropriate, and why', in order to guide their conversation.
- Focus on student ability to evaluate the content and metacognitive strengths of different answers.

Talking Heads
What

In talking heads, students are presented with around a half dozen alternative answers to a question. In this scenario, the question answered is most certainly not a 30-mark history essay, but perhaps a quick 4-mark question around the structure of a diamond. The purpose of this strategy is for students to focus on the specificity of the different answers, especially the key words that are used in each response, in order to determine which answers are superior to the others. In this strategy, the answers provided are often shown as speech bubbles coming from different individuals, hence the strategy name of 'talking heads'.

When/How

This is another strategy that you will be able to incorporate into most lessons, especially where students are beginning to become comfortable with content. As with many strategies where students do not yet have a strong understanding of the subject specific content, they would not be able to successfully complete the metacognitive elements of this strategy.

Unfortunately, much like the good, better and best answers strategy, this strategy does require a bank of resources to be built up. It may be that you, or members of your faculty, have them already, but most likely it will require you to produce your own different talking head scenarios for a range of different questions. Again, consider how you can split up the planning amongst members of your faculty and share your end resources.

Why

The comparison of good, better and best answers only really works for longer answers, where students are trawling through many lines of calculations of points and evidence to deduce what makes one answer better than another. However, sometimes we just need to focus on those shorter 2–6-mark questions that often get overlooked for analysis of those longer questions. Not only that, but this strategy allows us to focus on the specific vocabulary, and the structure of higher-quality shorter answers. Students will be evaluating why some vocabulary is superior to others, and why the structure or explanation given by one answer is clearer and more concise than another. Overall, this evaluation should support student understanding when they go and attempt these sorts of questions themselves.

Examples

During science lessons, I love to use the talking heads strategy for description questions of around 4–6 marks in length. The reason that I like to use it for descriptive questions is so that students are able to focus on concise but effective descriptions. I find that too often students fail to provide sufficient depth to their answers, or are not sufficiently concise in their writing.

Students work in small groups of three or four. They are provided with up to six alternative 'talking head' options, and need to determine which of the options is the superior answers.

With the options, it is imperative that it is not obvious which answer is the best. Equally, for a 6-mark question, I also ensure that one answer would not get one mark, one answer get two marks (and so forth), as again, this would be too easy.

Instead, many of the answers provide the same content, but in different levels of explanation, clarity and conciseness, so that students can determine the best write-up of the answer. It would be fair to conclude that this has not necessarily improved students' recall of the key subject knowledge, but it has certainly improved students' understanding of effective, concise and clear answers.

Summary

- Provide 'talking heads' – different answers/opinions for shorter questions – around 2–6 marks long.
- Get students to identify factors that make answers superior to one another.
- Focus on key vocabulary and answer structure to support students' own attempts at these short mark questions.

Exam Question Marking

What

This strategy is very similar to that of good, better and best answers. However, rather than just giving students three pre-marked pieces of work that you have identified as being similar in levels, in this strategy students have to do the marking and grading themselves. As with the previous strategy, select possibly two or three different answers that you want students to have a look at, most likely with each answer displaying one particularly impressive part, such as clear definitions, accurate recall of facts or concise explanation. Provide and train students with a given mark scheme, and then allow students to mark the answers themselves, assigning a total mark for the answer, and a grade where appropriate. At this point, subject-specific understanding should have improved. To build on this, get students to discuss their marking – what mark have they given, and why? Where have they given marks, and where have they not? Are there differences in where these marks have been awarded?

This strategy is of course very similar to moderation that we might do after a set of mock exams within our faculties. I am sure that most faculties will sit down to consider the marks that they have given, if they match up, if certain aspects have been awarded marks by one teacher and not another, and why this might be. This is a crucial exercise for us as staff – not just to ensure standardisation of marking, but also as continuous professional development (it is often said that the best form of CPD for teachers is to become an exam marker). If, then, this exercise is so important to our own understanding of accurate marking and evaluation, we surely want students to have these skills, too?

When/How

This is not going to be a strategy that you bring out on a highly frequent basis. Not only will it take quite a lot of time to get answers together, but it is a strategy that will take a longer time to do successfully. For longer exam answers, then, it is likely that this would take up a whole teaching period.

Once you have decided on an appropriate time to utilise this strategy – again, likely once students have mastered the content required – provide students with a clear and understandable mark scheme (you will probably need to amend an exam board mark scheme), and take some time to explain to students which features will earn the answer marks. Once you are confident that students have at least a base level of understanding of this mark scheme, then you can let them loose. Give students a time limit to firstly mark the answer (our answers) that you have given them. Once this time is up, provide students with another specified block of time for them to discuss the marks that they have given, and why they have given those marks. It may be appropriate for you to guide this conversation by getting students to go through each part of the mark scheme in turn, by providing sample questions or discussion points on the board, or through modelling a conversation with a student in front of the class first, so that students are aware of what their discussion should resemble. It would also probably be wise to bring all students back together at the end of their discussion period, and get the opinions of different students. Here, you are probably going to choose students who you have identified as making well-supported points when you have been walking around the classroom, allowing other students to be exposed to high-quality points and explanations. Where a firm mark or grade can be assigned to an answer, it would be very wise to share this with students. Explain to students how this mark or grade has been determined, and possibly (time permitting) explore what the answer needs to receive a higher mark or grade, and/or what the answer includes to reach that mark or grade, rather than a slightly lower mark or grade. If you have discussed this question previously within a faculty meeting, it would also be highly beneficial to discuss with students the conversations that you had with other faculty members and where alternative opinions over grading may have arisen from.

Why

As mentioned in the beginning part of this strategy, exam-marking analysis is something that would often form part of high-quality subject-specific professional development, faculty meetings, and general conversations with colleagues. Understanding a mark scheme, and how this applies to an answer, and therefore determining a mark or grade to award an answer, is not just a hugely difficult skill, but also crucial to being able to provide effective and accurate feedback to our students. However, as our students get older, we want, or rather need, them to be able to evaluate their own work, and to determine whether they have met the expectations of the question, or not. Where students have a 10-mark question, and a mark scheme, we need students to be able to identify how well they have done against the mark scheme. Of course, students are not subject experts, and so they are unlikely to be extremely accurate. However, with a little bit of training, using this strategy, they are likely to be within the ball-park of the answer or grade for a question, which will allow them to self-evaluate their progress, and areas for development (as well as areas of strength). If students are ignorant of what a high-grade, medium-grade, or low-grade answer looks like, they will be unaware of the quality of their answers, and their self-reflection and evaluation will be lacking. If we can upskill students so that they can interpret a mark scheme and begin to evaluate their own answers, they will be in a far stronger position.

Moreover, this strategy is incredibly helpful in supporting student's subject knowledge. Many of the strategies within this book will of course support subject knowledge, either directly or indirectly, but this strategy will probably help more than others: an added bonus.

Examples

To prepare students for their final performance, we engage in two different types of practice. Firstly, we isolate the skills they require to be successful and deliberately practise them. We then rehearse. Through the rehearsal, we replicate the performance's 'complexity and uncertainty' (Lemov et al., 2012). In maths the performance is an examination.

As part of the students' rehearsal process will include model answers of examination questions, I would show the work of a student, using the Teach Like a Champion technique Show Call (Lemov, 2015). Depending on how far through the rehearsal we were, the example could be from a student in the class or, if we are at the beginning of the process and the students are yet to engage in their purposeful practice, this could be staged or be collected from a source outside of the class. In the Show Call, I explicitly narrate where the marks lie and what the examiner report said about the success students had in picking up these marks. The Show Call will conclude with a fully narrated, full-mark response that is visible for the students. The narration in the response will use colours to highlight links and key points, exploring where marks could be lost and why. This would include exam technique advice. For example, if the question says that you must show all your working, full marks will not be awarded for a correct answer only. After modelling the process of answering an exam question, I would ask the students to deliberately practise answering similar exam questions themselves.

The deliberate practice would be followed by some more purposeful practice where students would use the Teach Like a Champion technique Everybody Writes (Lemov, 2015). Students would be given a set of answers that were given to an examination question. These could be real examples or could be designed based on teacher experience and knowledge for what the common misconceptions might be. The students would be asked to mark and annotate the work, describing in full sentences where the marks should be awarded and why. They would also be asked to write about what marks were not awarded and what stopped the awarding of those marks. Students would be asked to write an exam report for examination questions at the end of this exercise, commentating on the misconceptions that students showed when answering the question and describing how well the question might have been answered. This could be something that students write before the exercise as a prediction so that they could see if the misconceptions they thought might occur were actually the misconceptions seen in the examination responses. Students would discuss their reflections publicly and I would build on their ideas or challenge them, thinking about what is the same and what is different in each of their responses.

This technique could be used in a variety of ways, in a variety of scenarios. I have seen the technique of asking students to mark an exam question work successfully with answers that require extended writing. Students could engage in comparative marking, where they look at answers and comment on which answer is better and why. Students could use their own work to reflect upon and redraft their answer. The technique could be used as part of a re-teach or as a way of introducing examination practice.

Students could engage in the Teach Like a Champion technique, Turn and Talk or they could work independently. Every student may see one exam question with different answers to compare or there may be a series of questions that are linked and get progressively more challenging. Whatever the design, asking students to mark an exam piece of work and consider what an examiner report might look like is powerful in knowing what makes a 'great' exam question answer so that the students can produce their own 'great' answers in their own future performances.

Dave Tushingham

Summary

- Provide students with an exemplar answer and mark scheme (which is unlikely to be the exam mark scheme, as this is too complex).
- With the given (adapted) mark scheme, provide students with an allotted time to mark work within their groups.
- Develop a discussion around the marks given and why they were given. Perhaps take time to compare to your own marking, so students can understand exactly where marks would be awarded.

Strategy Justification and Evaluation

What

This strategy would be put into place once students have already attempted a task or a question. Once students have done this, they would then come together in their groups, and discuss their own attempts at the task. This discussion would revolve around two different points. Firstly, which strategy did the student choose and why, and secondly, what is their evaluation of this strategy use? Would the student use this strategy again? What went well, and what did not go well?

When/How

This strategy could only be utilised after students have completed a task or question, which could have been completed using at least two different strategies. If there is just one strategy that students could (or would) use to complete a task, then there would not be too much to discuss! You will also need to ensure that students will use a variety of different strategies, and do not just revert to the same one. Again, this would not be great for discussion. One way to ensure that students have all utilised different strategies is through assigning each student with a particular strategy to use. For example, if there are four 'reasonable' strategies that students could use, place students in groups of four, and each student will use one of the four different strategies identified.

Considering these requirements, it is clear that this is not going to be a strategy that you will use all of the time. It is not just because most tasks we give to students can only be approached in one particular way, but also that students will typically all revert towards one strategy, or, due to limited curriculum time, you may have only modelled one specific strategy in detail. Therefore, in your long-term planning, consider where students will be exposed to two or more strategies in equal amounts, and are likely to use a variety of different approaches.

In order for this strategy to succeed, providing students with a range of sentence starters or key points would help scaffold a successful discussion. These questions would include:

- Which strategy did you use, and why?
- Would you use this strategy again if you repeated the task?
- What are the strengths and weaknesses of the strategy that you used?

Additional questions could also be put in as you see fit, and may vary depending on the topic or task that students have just approached.

Why

Students are more likely to be successful where they have a range of different strategies that they can use, and will use at appropriate times. In order for students to be aware of a range of strategies, and an appropriate time to use each, not only do they need to be exposed to questions and tasks where alternative strategies can be used, but they also need to be provided with an opportunity to evaluate the appropriateness of these different strategies. Through developing a discussion around this, students will be able to explore the appropriateness of not just the strategy that they chose, but also of alternative strategies (that they decided against) that other students did use. Through using this strategy, students will be able to explore the pros and cons of several strategies very quickly, without having to re-attempt the same task several times with each of the different strategies in turn.

Additionally, students will also improve their reasoning and justification skills through this task. Students will need to self-evaluate and justify the strategy that they have used, and then discuss and argue this out with other group members. The overall outcome is improved understanding of strategy appropriateness, but unintended positives include reasoning and justification.

Examples

This strategy is the perfect one for a mathematics classroom, where students are exposed to multiple alternative strategies on a frequent basis. Within any mathematics topic, there will always be multiple ways to go about completing the task, and therefore multiple strategies are continuously generated.

However, students often have their own preferred way of completing a problem – typically utilising the strategy that they are most comfortable with, rather than the one that is most effective for the given task. Therefore, utilising this strategy, students would complete a given task, and then move to work in groups where they would discuss the strategy that they had chosen. Within these discussions, students should not be focusing on how their strategy worked, but rather why they chose that strategy and how it worked out for them; that is, was the strategy as effective as they thought it would be prior to beginning the task. As with many of the strategies mentioned in this book, this strategy allows students to consider alternative approaches without having to complete the task over and over again with alternative strategies. Therefore, students get all of the information and evaluation of strategies that they need, without having to complete the task many times over.

Summary

- Once students have completed a task, they must form pairs or groups to discuss the strategies that they used.
- Each student needs to be able to explain the strategy they used, the strengths and weaknesses of it, and how their approach would change next time (if it would at all).
- This strategy allows students to have a thorough understanding of each strategy, without having to complete the same task with numerous different strategies.

Goal-Free Problems

What

Goal-free problems, successfully used more frequently within mathematics over the past few years, present students with typical exam question information, but do not present a specific question that needs to be answered or a task that needs to be attempted. Students therefore are given free rein over what they want to calculate, and the direction that they wish to take with the information that they have been provided. Within groups, students are able to discuss the alternative strategies that they can employ, as well as the answers that they get. Students will also be able to discuss and determine which strategy or strategies are most effective for manipulating the information that they have been given, as well as the values and ideas they managed to determine.

When/How

The goal-free problem has multiple uses within the classroom, and as a homework task too. Primarily the goal-free problem would be used when students have completed a topic and have mastered all of the content, skills and strategies that they require. At this point, students will be able to approach this type of task and, hopefully, begin to explore multiple different avenues given the information that they have been provided with.

Alternatively, the goal-free problem could be a good way to introduce a topic, especially if students have some level of knowledge of the topic area, perhaps through overlaps within units or if it has been covered in a previous key stage. Through using a goal-free problem, you can explore the multiple different avenues of a topic right at the beginning, allowing students to see a range of strategies that will be required for the topic, as well as the range of avenues that they will be able to take given the information within an exam.

Furthermore, the goal-free problem provides a fantastic revision task. Not only does it provide students with exam practice and the challenge of recalling information previously taught, but it also has very low barriers to just attempt, well, something. Given a large amount of information, such as angles in a mathematics problem question, students will be able to attempt something. This also makes it a brilliant homework task. We know students can use the slightest confusion with a task as a reason to not attempt the work. By removing all of these barriers, you hopefully have a task that all students will be able to attempt to some extent. Furthermore, if you are a practitioner or school that employs flipped learning, this task would allow students to explore all theories, ideas, formulas and so forth, in an easily accessible format prior to the lesson.

Why

Goal-free problems allow students to explore the content of an entire topic area without the pressure of a specific question or task. Students get the opportunity to consider all of the different information that they can calculate or discuss, thus better preparing them for problem-solving questions with a narrower focus in future. Moreover, students will also be able to practise their range of strategies developed within a topic on the given goal-free problem, allowing them to evaluate the effectiveness of different strategies given variation of information given within a problem.

Examples

A group of pupils are given some 'goal-free' information that involves the prices of different food and drinks at a café. The teacher's aim of the lesson is specifically to develop problem-solving skills, particularly helping those pupils who rarely know which calculations are required in mixed-word problems. This is a class who have been regularly exposed to word problems but that mainly fit the unit of work; that is, if they are learning about multiplication then they do word problems using multiplication. The teacher asks the class to write a question initially that involves addition using the prices. There then follows paired discussion into why addition is required to solve their problems. There is no emphasis put on finding the answer. The task is repeated but pupils are asked to write a question each for subtraction, multiplication and division. Once some of the other questions have been discussed, they can then be mixed up and sorted by pupils, through group or paired discussion, into those requiring each type of calculation.

The teacher can assess the reasons that pupils are struggling to identify the question types much more effectively as discussion is based around the problem structure, rather than around how an answer was reached.

Some pupils who find this easy are then asked to write multi-step questions which are shared with their peers.

A class of mixed-ability pupils are given a diagram showing the distances on a train journey between two end destinations. They are asked to write a question on their mini-whiteboard based on the information that they are given. Pupils write questions which involve a wide range of mathematical concepts. The teacher then asks pupils to hold up their board if they think that they have a question that requires a certain type of calculation. These pupils are invited to the front of the classroom where the rest of the class can identify what is the same and what is different about the problems shown. The teacher then selects some of the problems and pupils are asked to rank them by difficulty, explaining why they have been ordered in that way. Again, no answers have been calculated as the focus is on the structure of the problem. Their questions are then compiled to use in the next lesson, and, because the children are now very familiar with the information given, they have much better comprehension as well as a sense of ownership.

Top tips

Modelling is key. Demonstrate the thinking process and insist that no answers are required. This means they will focus more on the information. For those who find word problems difficult it significantly reduces the cognitive load, as they can explore the problem rather than become anxious about finding an answer that others around them may have already completed, which can be demotivating.

Goal-free problems that involve graphs or geometry also work well. Pupils spend longer looking at titles and labels to understand the data displayed when they don't have a question to answer, as well as identifying the properties of geometrical diagrams.

Use images instead of words for younger pupils or those where reading is a barrier. A photo showing a real-life setting, such as a plate of cakes, gives a familiar context. An adult can scribe the pupils' ideas and support them in formulating questions. Stem sentences are also useful for supporting those who would benefit from a scaffold.

Try gluing the information/image in the centre of a large piece of paper so that small groups of children can work around it. This means that the whole group can access it, adding individual questions or pooling their ideas.

Ask pupils to write a question that cannot be answered from the given information. This can be used to discuss why it is not possible and what extra information is required to be able to answer it. This gives valuable perception into pupils' thinking and understanding.

To challenge pupils, ask them to write a 'tricky' question using the given information. What is the hardest question that you could give your friend to solve? The intention is not to produce a long-winded, complicated 'story', but something that may involve several steps of calculation or requiring the use of other known facts around measures, for example.

Impact

After a short amount of time, with regular use, the impact on pupils' problem-solving skills is very noticeable. Those pupils who previously juggled the numbers in a question into a calculation with little understanding of what they were doing or who skimmed the details are now much better at comprehending the information and thinking about problems more as stories. Confidence increases as the flexibility in producing individual problems has produced valuable mathematical talk. This talk is much more of a useful insight for the teacher, as well as being able to identify mis-conceptions linked to vocabulary. Those pupils who used to give up very quickly, are now spending much more time reading and looking at the information given which has developed a greater degree of resilience. Those who usually solve problems easily are pushed out of their comfort zone and being challenged by the question writing, rather than often being focussed on having the answer first, which can demotivate other pupils.

Alison Hogben

Summary

- Goal-free problems allow students to explore the full content of a topic without the barrier of a specific question or task.
- Students can attempt to calculate as many values and formulate as many different ideas as possible given the information provided.
- Students can compare the strategies that they use, including their effectiveness, as well as the values and ideas that they managed to calculate/formulate.

Problem-Solving Grids
What

These problem-solving grids, shown below, have been created and adapted from the great work of Mevarech (yes, them once again). As a mathematician, these grids are perfect for my subject, and also that of science, and often technology, too. However, as a subject expert yourself, you may also find uses for them, or adaptations, which ensure they suit non-science, technology, engineering and mathematics (STEM) subjects as well.

The problem-solving grid provides a template for students to utilise when they are progressing through a problem. The idea here is that students will be given a template per group, and collaboratively need to go through the four different sections, and complete each in a suitable amount of depth (too much depth, and this is no longer a planning tool as is the aim).

When/How

I would urge the use of problem-solving grids to be in each and every lesson (where possible and suitable). This is why having multiple copies all laminated and ready to go with a whiteboard pen is so beneficial – you can get them out quickly and easily to students without having to panic that you had not copied enough sheets for that day. The main reason why these grids should be used so frequently, however, is due to the huge benefits that they can bring to your students, in an area (problem solving) where they are typically so weak – though this is explored in greater detail below.

When first using these problem-solving grids, I would use the highly scaffolded versions, so that students are clear on what each of the four stages is referring to. This will allow students to focus on the content that they have recorded, rather than what they need to be doing with the problem-solving grid. Over time, as students become more confident with the grid, you can gradually move them to the less scaffolded versions.

What is brilliant about these grids as well is that they force students to record key notes. This will then add a depth and richness to a whole class-discussion as students have written contributions.

Why

Students are typically very poor at problem solving (Ofsted, 2015). Evaluation work from Mevarech shows that there are things that we can do to support students' problem-solving abilities, in part, by ensuring students take time to comprehend,

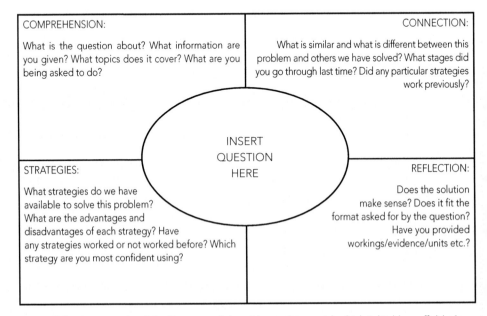

Figure 7.3 An example of the Frayer model problem-solving grid, which is highly scaffolded, ensuring students understand the comments that they need to record in each section

consider connections, decide upon strategy options and then evaluate their work once it is complete. Therefore, this grid will ensure that students are working through these four stages, and by working in groups, students will get the support that they need to complete tasks successfully. Furthermore, as students become more confident with the grid, they can move away from using it in groups to using it in pairs, and then individually.

You will also notice that there are different scaffolded levels of the grid, as shown in the diagrams. This allows you to gradually withdraw the scaffold from students as they show you that they, firstly, are clear on what the four different stages are, and then that they are working through these four stages when they are problem solving.

Overall, therefore, the problem-solving grids force students to use a strategy that research shows is hugely successful at addressing an area that students are typically so poor at. What's not to love?

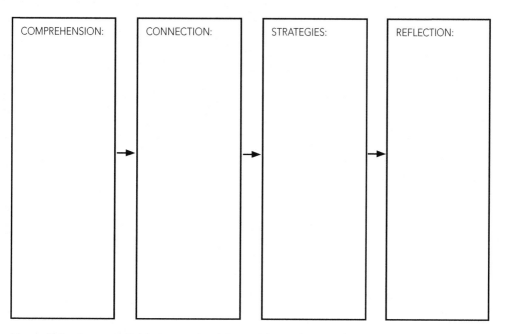

Figure 7.4 A non-scaffolded example of the problem-solving grid

Examples

The metacognitive exam question grid was created to engage students with metacognitive reflection, which is directly linked to their GCSE exam questions, and to create a structure that can be used regularly within lessons to allow students to track their own progress. The creation of the grid stemmed from underperformance in mock exams compared to exam questions within classes, and the need for students to understand why there was a difference and how to improve. The focus on exam question types also means that the grid aims to further embed students' knowledge of exam structures and rubric.

The grid structure was chosen to provide students with a step-by-step guide to metacognitive thinking (Webb, 2021) with a specific focus on a particular exam question type – the open title box means it can be used for multiple exam questions without creating a specific grid for each question type. The nature of the step-by-step guide is to break down students' metacognitive thinking into clear categories and ensure that each box has prompts and tips to support explicit strategy instruction which Kistner et al. (2010) found was the most beneficial technique for developing metacognitive skills.

The grid focusses on using explicit metacognitive language outlined in the EEF's 2018 guide to metacognition and the questions in the planning, monitoring and evaluating boxes have been constructed from their guidance. The planning box has been further informed by Ellis et al.'s 2014 research on evaluating consistent practice with links to previous learning to ensure that students can evaluate their progression over time with each exam question type. The inclusion of an exam rubric box is linked to the focus of the research on exam performance and the EEF guidance (2018) to explicitly teach pupils how to organise their learning; through recalling the key exam question structures, this will prompt their recall of specific targets and skills to improve.

Table 7.1 Description

Exam Question:	
Exam Rubric: What is the exam question asking you to do? Consider the specific question and question structure.	**Planning:** Based on previous exam questions, what do you need to focus on for this question?
Monitoring: What have you done successfully in this exam question? Have you improved on your area of focus? How?	**Evaluating:** What are your next steps with this type of exam question? Set a new focus or add more depth to a continued focus.

Rachel Cliffe

Summary

- Provide students with the available problem-solving grids. The level of scaffolding on the grid can vary depending upon students confidence, abilities and experience with these grids.

- In their groups, students then need to work through a problem or task, whilst utilising the grid. This grid will ensure that students stay on track, and are drawing on key information, such as connections with similar problems that they have done recently.
- This strategy should see greater resilience and improved outcomes with problem solving.

Summary

- Some discussion strategies require a little more planning, preparation and experience than other metacognitive strategies. Take time to build up your experience and confidence with lower threshold discussion strategies before branching out!

Further Reading

Below are readings which explore some of these more unfamiliar metacognitive strategies:

Sandringham Research School (2018). 'Graphic Organisers', Sandringham Research School, available at: https://researchschool.org.uk/sandringham/news/graphic-organisers (accessed 7 May 2022)

Sealy, C. (2022). 'Goal Free Problems and Focused Thinking: How I Wish I'd Taught Primary Maths', Third Space Learning, available at: https://thirdspacelearning.com/blog/how-teach-primary-maths-goal-free-question/ (accessed 7 May 2022)

Thorsen, E. (2017). 'Odd One Out: A Strategy to Get Students Thinking Critically in Any Subject', Teaching with Elly Thorsen, available at https://ellythorsenteaching.blogspot.com/2017/01/odd-one-out-strategy-to-get-students.html#:~:text=It%20is%20generally%20used%20as,think%20critically%20about%20a%20topic (accessed 7 May 2022)

8
Successful Implementation

Learning Objectives

In this chapter we will:

- Explore the key factors that you need to consider to successfully implement metacognitive strategies in your classroom
- Begin to consider the factors that you need to consider as a leader implementing metacognition on a wider scale.

Introduction

The importance of this chapter cannot be underestimated. For all the goodwill and determination in the world, if you are not clear on how you are going to implement these strategies, you are not going to be successful. I think that this is often an overlooked part of CPD and initial teacher training (ITT). We are so often provided with these new shiny strategies and told to go and use them because they have so much positive impact, but we very rarely have the opportunity to consider how we are going to implement these strategies successfully.

Therefore, this chapter is broken down into ten different areas for you to consider when implementing metacognition in the classroom. Hopefully, these will provide you with the guidance and thinking points that you require to be successful with some hugely powerful strategies.

Revise, Revise, Revise

Before beginning to implement any metacognitive strategies successfully, you need to make sure that you understand the theory inside out. As stated right at the start of this book, you can implement these strategies, but you will be implementing them better if you truly understand what metacognition is and what we are looking to develop with students. This is much like generally teaching, anyway. Where we are not confident with the content that we are delivering in a lesson, we will probably still be able to deliver it, but we will not be able to deliver it in the best way possible. We would miss out on key subtle points to draw out, or key threshold questions that we need to ask students to ensure understanding. So yes, we could teach it, but just not all that well. Metacognition is exactly the same. Yes, we can use these metacognitive strategies, but we will not be getting the full benefit out of them.

So, make sure that you are familiar with the history and development of metacognition. Are you clear on the metacognitive processes? Are you clear that metacognition is 'invisible' and our aim is to make it 'visible'? Only once you are clear and confident on these points should you attempt to implement.

Pick a Suitable Class

As ever when we are looking to implement new strategies, remove as many potentially barriers as possible. Above we looked at removing the barrier of not being confident with the theory, and here, you need to consider removing the barrier of difficult, or at least less easy, classes. When you are implementing these new strategies, you need the class to give you the space and time to try out these new ideas. If you have a class that just seems to burst into chatter as soon as you stop talking, or a group that breaks down at the first challenge outside of their comfort zone, then these are probably not the correct groups to be choosing to try out your new strategies (even if they are the groups who you believe need these strategies the most). Rather, choose that group who will be patient, and have a little more resilience. This will mean that you can make mistakes, rephrase questions and reattempt tasks without having to worry yourself with behaviour. This will allow you to iron out difficulties and flaws with your delivery and these tasks before you take them to those more 'difficult' classes who really need these strategies more than others.

Consider What the Weaknesses Are

Before you even begin to implement a strategy, you first need to understand where the difficulties or weaknesses of a group are. It is worth deciding these after you have decided which group you are going to use as guinea pigs as well, otherwise you will decide on a strategy and then find that it is not relevant to the group that you are trying it out on.

Metacognition is a wide field, as the strategies in this book have shown. Equally, the strategies within this book go from those you can begin to implement for complete novices (such as your own modelling focusing on metacognitive processes), to those where a little bit of know-how is needed (for example, the problem-solving grids if being used individually or without scaffolding). Therefore, it is crucial that you zone in on the area that you want to work on with your chosen class. Make sure that you decide which of the four areas – processes, modelling, questioning, discussion – you are going to focus on. Which of these areas do your class struggle with the most, or where do you want them to improve in particular? Once you have decided this, draw up an aim before you choose a strategy. For example, do you want to improve students' knowledge of strategy choice, or understanding of the mechanics of a strategy, or how strategies can work better or less well depending on the question (notice the similarities, but also subtle differences between these aims)? Each of these individual aims may also have a different strategy associated with them, as well. For improving student choice of strategy choice, you might use the questioning strategy of 'compare strategies, plans and answers'. For understanding the mechanics of a strategy, you might use the modelling strategy 'strategy comparison'. Meanwhile, to focus on how strategies work well or less well, you may wish to utilise the discussion strategy of 'find someone who', where students discuss with another student who has used an alternative strategy for the same problem.

You can see here the intricacies of choosing a strategy. Remember as well that this is an art, and not a science. Well, it's mainly science, but there is some subjectivity left, too. Make sure, therefore, that you are happy that the strategy you choose supports students in improving the area that you are targeting, and do not just choose a strategy because you want to try it out. An analogy for this is the worksheet in class. How many times do we see a superb worksheet, perhaps with great layout, some superb examples or some great questions? However much we may wish to use this worksheet, it is only appropriate to use it if it is going to help students make progress towards the learning aim of the lesson they are in. If that worksheet does not help, then students will not be achieving that aim. Choosing a metacognitive strategy is the same. Choose one that sounds awesome, but is not appropriate to address the area you have chosen, and that area will not get addressed. However, do not panic if you choose the incorrect strategy. That is why you have chosen a nice class to do it with, remember.

Consider Your Resources

Most of the strategies within this book are designed to be low workload. Many require a change in approach to activities that we are already doing, such as modelling or questioning, whilst some require a one-time preparation, such as laminating some problem-solving grids, and then you are good to go every time. However, when you have chosen the strategy, ensure that you begin to consider straight away the resources that you may need. I would not suggest leaving this until printing day, or the free period before you are using this strategy. Get ahead of yourself if you can, and again remove as many barriers (in this scenario, last-minute stress) as you can. This will give you the head space to be focusing on the high-quality use of this strategy, rather than the last-minute panic of realising that you have not got the resources. Remember, resources do not just mean your printed sheets either. It includes your scripted questions or planned out modelling that you may wish to do in preparation for using these strategies.

Script Your Lines

Briefly mentioned above, scripting your lines is a great way to give yourself that much-needed boost of confidence, and increase the chances of early success with your newly selected metacognitive strategy. Scripting is often a strategy used by early-career teachers, who do not have the experience of having taught each topic thoroughly several times, and perhaps do not know how to clearly explain something, or deal with a behavioural issue in the heat of the moment with a quick one-liner. This is where scripting comes in. If you have key lines or phrases that you want to use – because you know they are clear, concise and specific – then you will be onto a winner. It is the same with these metacognitive strategies. If you are an early-careers teacher, you'll be familiar with scripting and the power that it brings. If you are a more experienced teacher, scripting will ensure that you stay focussed on the metacognition, rather than reverting back to those lines that you have honed over your years of teaching.

Overall, it cannot harm to script a few key lines that you want to cover when introducing your strategy. If you are going down the scripting route, then make sure to do this in good time as, again, considering your script two minutes before the students walk through the door is possibly not the best situation to be in. Equally, once you have completed the lesson, take time to evaluate how your script went, and tweak it so it is improved for the next time you are using that strategy (evaluation, see!).

Short-Term Planning

Though these strategies have been made as straightforward as they possibly could, they still maintain the need for some planning and consideration. This is also true of planning when to utilise these strategies. If you have decided on a class and strategy, and you have the resources ready to go, this is great. However, if you have not identified a suitable point to introduce this strategy, you either are not going to do it, or it is not going to go very well. In short, metacognition will not happen by accident.

When you are choosing the strategy and group, you also need to be considering the first time it will be suitable to utilise this strategy. Have you ensured that you have taught all of the required content students need in order to access these strategies? Are you confident that students are in suitable places for group work? Have you explored alternative strategies sufficiently to allow for a whole-class discussion on their utility? Again, when you are choosing a strategy, it should jump out to you when you can use it. Make sure that you mark these clearly in your lesson sequencing, and that you only begin to use the strategy when the criteria above (and any others you can think of) have been met, so that it is more than likely going to be successful.

Long-Term Planning

As well as short-term planning for the use of a strategy, you also need to consider the long-term planning. Rome was not built overnight, and neither will change to your teaching practice, or student metacognitive abilities either. Therefore, after you have utilised a strategy once, keep considering where it would be appropriate to use it again, and again, and again. You may be wondering why you need to do this, but there are two key reasons. Firstly, you need the opportunity to keep using the strategy and refine your practice. Without you practising with these strategies, it is never going to be as effective as it could, linking to the first point in this list. The more you practise, the better you will get at using the strategy and repeating the reward. Secondly, students also need to get familiar with the strategy that you are using. Much like yourself, the first time they encounter a new planning grid, or weird questions about 'something called process', they are also going to be a little lost. Therefore, students need to encounter the same strategy several times until they are familiar and confident with it. This is especially true for new vocabulary, such as 'knowledge of self', or how to successfully use some of the templates, such as the problem-solving grids.

It would also probably be wise to work on one strategy until you are happy it is embedded. If you get to stage 6 and then are also working on another couple of strategies at stages 2 and 3 in this list, you might be spreading yourself too thinly. Make sure you cement one strategy, and begin to apply it to those trickier classes, before you go on and start developing the use of other strategies. Also remember that the more strategies that you learn, the quicker you will pick them up, as you will be more confident with the theory and know more of the pitfalls that you could encounter.

Get Some Feedback

One of the reasons that the early-careers framework was updated, and covered the recently qualified teacher year, is because of the drop-off in support that some teachers could feel once they had lost that formal mentor, whom they maybe had a meeting with once a week or fortnight, and who would frequently drop in to do partial or full lesson observations and provide feedback. However, ECT or not, the power of feedback is huge, and would be greatly beneficial to all when delving into this metacognitive journey.

At this stage, you should be clear on the thinking that you are wanting students to improve, and the strategy that you are wanting to use to lead this improvement. Therefore, you have a very clear aim and a very clear strategy. Share this with a trusted colleague, and, where possible, arrange for them to come into class and observe you utilising the model. There are many positives to this process, but two obvious ones. Firstly, you will get clear feedback on how well you did with implementing your new strategy. It does not matter whether the individual watching you is experienced with metacognitive practices or not, as you will have shared your aim and strategy with them beforehand,

and so they can assess you against this. The feedback that they are able to share with you could be extremely valuable in improving your metacognitive practice. Secondly, through allowing a colleague in to observe your new shiny strategy, you may inspire them and their teaching, as well. We know the power of these metacognitive strategies, and so being able to share them through high-quality modelling would be hugely satisfying for yourself, and beneficial for your colleague(s) and students more generally.

Compare to Your Aims

Whether you have a colleague come in to observe you or not, it will be crucial for you to sit down after implementation and consider how successful you have been. If we are talking the talk (metacognition is super-helpful), then we also need to walk the walk (I best be metacognitive myself). Self-evaluation is such a hard thing to do, because it seems to fall down to the bottom of our to-do list. There is always planning, or marking, or displays, or data, or something to do. However, our lives are significantly more difficult if we do not take the time to reflect and improve. Our lives would all be so much easier if behaviour was better and learning outcomes improved. If we do not take the time to reflect, they will not be. So, scope out some time, maybe the break or free period after you have used the strategy, to evaluate how successful you were. You can start from the question of, 'Have my students improved the weakness identified?', and work backwards from there. Take time to consider your explanations, the resources you used, and how you know students have made improvements (remember, metacognition is invisible, so how have you made it visible, and then also assessed for progress?). The first few times you use a strategy, you should also put in place some changes that will lead to you improving the next time that you utilise the strategy.

Take Your Time

Point ten is the most important of all of these points. Take. Your. Time. Introducing metacognitive strategies within your teaching is difficult, whether you are a newly qualified teacher or extremely experienced. Any change to our teaching is difficult, and it does take a long time to refine and cement it as a new habit. This all means, of course, that you need to give yourself time. Give yourself time to make mistakes. Give yourself time to make improvements. Give yourself time to confuse yourself and your students. Give yourself time to absolutely nail it.

The nine other points above may seem a little overwhelming, explaining how you should implement a strategy that could be as simple as showing two strategies side by side and narrating them as your model. However, there is so much depth in these points to ensure that difficulties and confusion faced by any teacher will be covered by the points mentioned above. So, if you have managed to stick with this chapter and read all of these points, great. Let them soak in, go and give it all a go, and then come back and look at these ten points again. Once you have given it a go a few times, you may re-read this chapter and different things may stand out to you.

Overall, try your best, give yourself a break if it all goes wrong and enjoy the power of these metacognitive strategies.

Further Examples

As well as my top tips, it is always interesting to get some insight from other practitioners.

Below are the thoughts of Rachel Cliffe, who has used metacognition extensively within her classroom practice.

Creating time for metacognition

After reflecting upon my own use of metacognition I found that I was using metacognition as an extension activity or rushing it at the end of the lesson. Consequently, students' reflections were stunted, rushed or not completed if they were still working on the main task. The quality of the reflections varied depending on the student and their effort which meant it was only really impacting on the efficient workers in the classroom. Since acknowledging the placement of metacognition within a lesson I have tried to create more time for the practice within my classroom; this includes placing exam practice questions at the start of the lesson and reflecting metacognitively afterwards, setting it as a specific standalone task, and if there is not enough time then replacing the reflections and re-visiting it at the start of the next lesson. Since allowing more time for metacognition the students' responses are of a higher quality and the practice is having a greater impact for all students.

Modelling metacognition

To create an atmosphere of resilience where students feel that they can openly admit their errors or acknowledge where improvements can be made, I have realised that as a teacher I need to be open and honest as well. One way I have tried to model metacognition is through the justification of tasks – explaining why they are completing the task, the intended impact and where applicable the challenges faced whilst creating the task. For example, whilst writing or annotating a modelled answer, I have aimed to use metacognitive language in the discussions and consider the strengths of the model, the areas to improve and how the model could be improved. Through making a conscious decision to consider my language and openness I found that afterwards I was more natural with including the vulnerability within my teaching.

Here, Lombardi and Goodwin discuss the implementation of metacognition across their school:

During 2021 a volunteer team of staff came together to discuss how research could be implemented across the whole school. Our aim, as part of the Research Hub, is to enable more staff to feel that they could engage with evidence-based inquiry. After many hours of discussion around what was missing from our school, what would benefit students and staff in a tangible way, we agreed that metacognition was the way forward. Most staff utilised metacognition already but were unable to put a name to it.

Metacognition is not a new fad, it has been around arguably since Ebbinghaus' Forgetting Curve of 1885. Our whole-school focus this academic year was assessment, retrieval practice and differentiation. This does not mean that we felt that staff are not spending time planning for this to occur in their classrooms; more that we wanted to ensure that they understood the reasons why. We took direction from the EEF's framework on implementation and sifted through many pages of research. We then delivered CPD on a whole-school basis that was grounded in evidence-based approaches, with implementable and tangible outcomes for our students.

> Every teacher needs to improve, not because they are not good enough, but because they can be even better. (Dylan Williams)

Within our Teaching and Learning meetings, we devised CPD sessions on some of the key practical uses of metacognitive approaches: encompassing why misconceptions are important, brain dumps and multiple-choice quizzes, all with a consideration for pupils with SEND needs. All three of these included evidence for them, ineffective practices and the benefits for students' recall. These were delivered live or sent out as handouts including research, should staff wish to delve deeper.

As part of our professional development cycles, we hold 'open door weeks', where staff were strongly encouraged to visit and share their own best practices around retrieval practice. Faculty meetings were given over to discussion around retrieval and metacognition. This occurred during directed time and did not require staff to complete anything above their normal workload. We know, as practising teachers, how important this is. The only exception to this was the implementation of an 8 a.m. optional half-termly Journal Club. This provided insight into how faculties could collaborate and overcome students' ineffective retrieval practices.

The flexibility of adding a few questions at any point in the lesson to check that knowledge has been embedded in the long-term memory is invaluable. The nuances of designing a good multiple-choice quiz are burdensome and we have highlighted this to staff. Are the answers closely related enough to encourage students to consider their answers and retrieve an answer but not too closely related to encourage misconceptions? Are the questions clearly written and free from distractors? Many of the quizzes from some of the popular sites are not so aware of these pitfalls. If the questions are not well written and the answers do not encourage retrieval of known facts, then are we really retrieving anything in a useful manner?

Something we did not cover, but we have been exploring, has been the use of metacognitively structured questions once an assessment has been completed, otherwise known as exam wrappers. Some of the Research Champions attended a webinar from Jennifer Webb who has included the use of these in her book *The Metacognition Handbook*. This is something that we would probably want to implement on a whole-school basis – having students consider questions, after the completion of an assessment, such as 'How confident did you feel before the assessment?', 'What do you wish came up?' and 'What score/grade do you think you have gained?'

Overall, we found that our biggest hurdle was how to approach cognitive science. Do you presume that an entire staff have no awareness of how learning happens in the brain? Do we spend years educating staff about how schema can be transferred to the long-term memory and into schemata? Part of this hurdle was the consideration given to time constraints and not wanting to over-burden staff with added workload.

This has been the inaugural year of our hub and we are excited to continue to champion metacognitive strategies and empower to staff to implement them.

Leadership

You may be sitting there as a head of department or assistant/deputy head teacher and wondering how you can instantly implement these strategies on a department or school-wide scale. This, in itself, could be a whole book altogether. However, it would be unfair not to cover any ideas at all in this book. Below, in significantly less detail than I would like, are some things that it would be worth considering as a leader when implementing metacognition across a department or school.

Main weaknesses

Whereas a teacher is focusing on the specific weakness of one of their teaching groups, if you were looking to introduce metacognition on a wider scale you would need to identify a common weakness shared by most or all students. You could perhaps identify weaknesses in Key Stage 3, for example, and separate weaknesses again in Key Stage 4. How you do this would be an in-depth project, and could range from assessments to book looks, observations to student voice panels. Either way, it would be a large and significant body of work that would need to be done right. What you cannot do is attempt to implement a large range of different strategies. To be successful, you would need to ensure that you have identified this key weakness, and choose a handful (with a maximum of three, perhaps) strategies that are suitable to address this weakness. You would then want all staff focusing on these handful of strategies at the same time to ensure consistency and the same diet of metacognitive strategies for students across the school. What you really can ill afford to do is have each teacher struggling away with their own strategy. Not only would teachers not have the support of colleagues, who would be focusing with their own strategy, but you will be overloading students, who would not become familiar with any of the strategies. So, keep it simple. Find the focus area, identify up to three strategies, and make sure that all staff are using them.

Training needs

You have read this book. You get the strategies. You know why you are doing them. But do staff? The very first point above was that when implementing metacognitive strategies, staff need to understand the theory to lead to the highest-quality implementation. Therefore, what are you going to do about this? How are you going to train staff on all of these strategies? Are you going to give up CPD time for metacognitive training (I'm available)? Are you going to buy a copy of this book for each member of staff (yes please)? Are you going to just hope for the best (do not do this)? As a leader, this is something that you are probably no stranger to. You will probably have introduced a range of strategies across a department and a school with great success. Just make sure that you treat this in the same way.

Consistent practice

When you do have staff using these metacognitive strategies around the building, you will need to ensure that there is consistency with what is happening. The easiest way to do this is by deciding upon some key features that all teachers must show in their practice. This means that teachers know what must be the same in every classroom, but also gives them a licence to put their own individual spin (personality, curriculum, experience) on the way that they deliver the strategy. You will find that by making these points of implementation clear, it will help you to evaluate what is happening across your school. Without having these points, what will you actually be looking for when you pop into classrooms? You need to make it so that everybody is clear on the key principles that they should be seeing, and making these as objective as possible. Where they are subjective, confusion will reign and you will not be able to ensure consistency across departments and across the school as a whole.

Do not rush

The last point for individuals implementing metacognitive strategies is to take their time. This is also true across a school. Implementing metacognitive strategies is not something that can happen overnight. It may be possible to successfully implement three strategies across a school during a term (not a half-term, a term), but any more strategies than this, or any less time than this, and they will either not be implemented correctly, or implemented sufficiently. Before you begin on your journey, it would be wise to consider a timeline for implementation. If you know what you are focusing on, how staff are going to be supported and what is happening in every classroom, what is your timeframe for having it all sewn up? If you have a timeframe to work to, you can monitor (those pesky metacognitive processes again) your progress, and see whether you are on track to meet your aims. These timeframes also stop you from being too overambitious, trying to get too much done too quickly, leading to burnt-out staff or poor (or pointless) implementation.

Do not stop there

The great thing about introducing metacognitive strategies is that it is a journey. There are so many strategies, and so much that you could look to implement. The more you successfully implement, the better the quality of teaching in your school and the more improved outcomes will be. Therefore, let metacognition be a journey for you and your department and/or school. Make it a running agenda item, or a one-per-month CPD session. You could even make it a staff performance management target. However you decide to, make sure that metacognition becomes an ingrained part of your department and your school. Your teaching and your students will be all the better for it.

Summary

- Ensure that you take time to consider how you are going to successfully implement your chosen metacognitive strategy. Do not get too excited with your shiny new technique without first ensuring a clear implementation plan.
- Make sure to remove as many barriers to implementation as possible, including being uncertain about metacognitive theory, difficult classes and the incorrect strategy for the specific class aim that you have.
- As a leader, ensure that you are training staff sufficiently, have a clear aim for student improvement and no more than three new strategies being implemented at once. Furthermore, ensure that you have a realistic timeframe for implementation too. Rush it, and it will all come crashing down.

Further Reading

To consider how best to implement metacognition in your own classroom, check out:

Burns, N. (2020). '5 Common Mistakes When Teaching Pupils How to Learn', *Tes*, available at: www.tes.com/magazine/archived/5-common-mistakes-when-teaching-pupils-how-learn (accessed 4 May 2022)

Cambridge International Education (2022). 'Getting Started with Metacognition', Cambridge International Education Teaching and Learning Team, available at: https://cambridge-community.org.uk/professional-development/gswmeta/index.html (accessed 4 May 2022)

Thompson, S. (2021). 'Metacognitive Strategies and Informing Language Learning – A Mid-Way Point Reflection', HISP Research School, available at: https://researchschool.org.uk/hisp/news/metacognitive-strategies-a-mid-way-point-reflection (accessed 4 May 2022)

For consideration on implementation more generally:

Education Endowment Foundation (2021). *Putting Evidence to Work: A School's Guide to Implementation*, EEF, pp. 1–48.

Evidence for Learning (2022). 'Implementation in Education', Evidence for Learning, available at: https://evidenceforlearning.org.au/evidence-informed-educators/implementation-in-education/#:~:text=Four%20major%20indicators%20of%20implementation,academic%20and%20behavioural)%20and%20teachers' (accessed 4 May 2022)

9

Metacognitive Homework and Independent Learning

Learning Objectives

In this chapter we will:

- Consider the importance of metacognitive homework
- Evaluate additional metacognitive approaches that could be used as homework tasks
- Consider the best approach to implementation.

Introduction

This chapter will focus on homework. To begin, the value of homework will be considered, before several pointers will be provided as to how current homework practices can be adapted to develop their metacognitive impacts. Finally, a range of additional strategies, which are all suitable for homework tasks, will be given.

Homework

Homework is a constant in school life. We all remember being set homework when we grew up, and we probably all set it weekly now, too. Regardless of whether we really believe in the benefits of homework, or just set it because it is school policy, it is something that we have to do. Therefore, if we are going to do it, we may as well do it as well as possible. Typically, homework focusses on developing in-school learning, often with additional repeat practice of the skill taught in class. There are other homework tasks that may be given too, such as knowledge organiser revision, flipped learning or online tasks. Though each of these types of homework task has their merits, this chapter will explore how you can develop metacognitive homework tasks, which, instead of focusing on the development of a specific subject specific concept, will look to develop a specific area of metacognition.

Move attention away from content, and place more emphasis on metacognitive practices

One of the biggest issues that we've all faced in teaching is students forgetting the content that you taught them in the previous lesson by the next time that you see them. How many times do we think that students have mastered some content, only to be shocked again that they all seem to have forgotten it? Such an issue is also true of revision. Whereas in class we are there to jog a student's memory about what we taught them previously, no such system exists when students are at home. If students cannot recall the content, for whatever reason, they thus are going to struggle massively on that piece of homework.

This is the main reason why I also support giving students homework on a content area that I know that they are confident with. By ensuring that students do recall the content required to complete a homework task, it removes a huge barrier to the competition of that task. However, this is not to say that I would recommend just providing students with work that you know they can do. If this were the case, that piece of homework would be completely pointless. Instead, this homework option provides us with a great opportunity to support the development of students' strategies – such as planning, monitoring and evaluation – with content that they are already familiar with.

For example, rather than providing students with a range of significantly more difficult equations to solve as their homework, simpler equations could instead be provided to students. Rather than placing emphasis on students completing a huge number of these, the homework task would instead be for students to attempt each of the, say, five equations, using at least two different methods. You can see here that students can access the work, as they all have at least one method to solve equations, but they are being forced to think about alternative strategies for the same question, as well as the utility and practicability of different strategies for different questions. Consequently, upon completion of this homework task, students would be significantly better at solving equations. Not through copious practice of more different question types, but through improving their knowledge of the different strategies that they have available to them, and when to use them.

This strategy would also work nicely at the end of a unit where multiple different strategies have been explored. Again, if we turn to mathematics, we can consider the solving of quadratic equations. In order to solve quadratics, students may need to factorise, or use the quadratic equation. Within factorising, students have two options, either to factorise into two brackets, or to complete the square. Within this topic, then, there are potentially three strategies that could be used for each question. This homework would therefore allow students to cement their understanding over which strategy to use when, and would be a brilliant precursor to a lesson-based discussion over the practicality and utility of each of the different methods. One particularly exciting discussion (as a mathematician) would be understanding which strategy students chose, and why, where all three strategies were options.

Building from these ideas, we can see that metacognitive flipped learning becomes an option. Flipped learning – where students learn the content required at home and then discuss and build on it within lesson, much like a university-type seminar – is not one I have ever or (I do not think) ever will advocate. My concerns arise from the fear of students embedding misconceptions within their own understanding due to self-teaching, which may not be unteachable within just a lesson or two back in school. Furthermore, getting students to do this effectively would be very hard to teach (could we all honestly reflect back on our own years at university and conclude that we always prepared effectively with pre-readings and research for lectures, seminars, discussions and so forth?). However, this strategy would be possible for metacognition, but only where these metacognitive strategies have already been used in class and students have been trained effectively at using them. Let us take, for example, the talking heads scaffold required for questioning or discussion activities within lessons. As discussed in the strategy chapters of this book, with this strategy students would consider the different answers, and form their own opinions on why some answers are better than others, and then be questioned on this, or discuss it within a group. With this idea of flipped metacognitive learning, students could instead be given this resource as their homework, alongside some directed questions, again potentially drawn from the strategy outlined in the earlier chapter. This would allow for homework to develop students' metacognitive abilities, force consideration of recently learnt knowledge and allow for greater preparation by students for future lessons, improving the quality of questioning, discussion and development of students, within school. A win, win, win, surely?

Ensure that students have the required subject knowledge that they need in order to be able to complete the task

It was highlighted extensively within the first part of this chapter that where homework contains content that students may struggle to recall, they are going to struggle to complete it. However, it has also been mentioned previously in this book that the careful use of scaffolds can support students' subject and metacognitive knowledge development. This is another area that homework can be tweaked in order to support improved outcomes – especially metacognitively.

If we consider the worst-case scenario for homework completion, we would all probably envisage a student sitting on the sofa, TV blaring and playing on their phone. We might also envisage a student who cannot remember the content required to complete the homework, does not have their book or another source of information to support them, and does not have a sibling, parent or family member who is either willing or able to support them. Unfortunately, for many students, one of these two scenarios is far too common. Therefore, how can we best support them, without giving students homework which is considerably too simple, or scrapping it all together?

Here, we need to be imaginative with the scaffolds that we can give to students when they're not physically sitting in front of us, as we cannot presume that they have access to any other resources (e.g. we cannot just provide them with a weblink for a helpful website when some students may not have Internet access). So, what could the scaffolding look like?

- Written examples and models – through providing students with clear step-by-step examples, they will have something to compare their new questions to, and a guide to help them to at least attempt this work. It at least removes one barrier of 'I had no idea where I needed to start'.

- Provide the problem-solving grid – the problem-solving grid is hugely beneficial with supporting problem solving, as it guides students through the four different areas of thinking which they need to go through to be successful. Therefore, if we placed different problems into the centre of the Frayer Model problem-solving grid, the grid itself would then provide the scaffold for students to begin working through the problem. At a minimum, the notes around the question, where students consider strategies that they could use or similar examples that they have completed previously, would shine a light on student thinking.

- Process graphics – one of the very first strategies mentioned in this book was the metacognitive process graphic, and how these ought to be put everywhere. This could also be on homework, again providing students with a little visual reminder of the different strategies that they should be going through when completing their work. Again, at worst, it provides a brief reminder to students and takes little more than ten seconds for us to do before printing off homework sheets.

- Utilise the metacognitive process planning sheets – once again, these metacognitive processes come popping back up. The reason for this is that they provide extremely clear, logical and linear stages for a student to move through with their approach to a task. Once again, by providing students with one of these process planning sheets, it provides a guide for them to work through when completing a problem. At a minimum, much like with the problem-solving grid above, it provides you with an insight into the approach that students took with the task, which ensures that the metacognitive thinking that a student is going through is now visible, and assessable, by yourself.

- Written reminders over good working environments – this may include instructions on the front page such as 'put your phone away', 'avoid talking to others' or 'work on this for 20 minutes without distraction'. This can help students to regulate their environment which we know they may otherwise not do. It also is going to support improved outcomes, merely by ensuring that students are working in a better environment than they would have been otherwise.

- Additional, standard scaffolds – whereas students may not have access to dictionaries, thesauruses, calculators and the like, we can provide students with banks of key words, alternative words, and required calculations and formulas (or maybe just a multiplication grid) to ensure that students do have a scaffold that they can utilise instantly. This is probably the closest type of scaffold to ones used in school, but also the one where students may need to be trained the most to use the scaffold effectively. Therefore, ensure whichever additional scaffold you are using with students is one that they are familiar with and have been trained to use. Otherwise, students are just going to have more information, and either not use it, or not know what to do with it. The more confusion generated, the worse. This strategy positively will also help to cement some of those in class scaffolds, with students becoming more familiar and confident using them if they are seeing them both in the classroom and also at home with their homework.

There will be dozens more scaffolds that you could put into place to support students with their homework, most of which will be subject and phase specific, and most of which will already be known to you. However, one important point of consideration is not just in providing students with a scaffolding and letting that be that. It is incredibly important to refer to the scaffold that you select to support students with their home-work. I would recommend that this is explored both when the homework is provided – especially where scaffolds provided are ones students need to be trained to use – as well as when homework is brought in and/or feedback given.

Consider some alternative metacognitive strategies

Strategies in this book so far have of course focussed around the four main areas of process, modelling, questioning and discussion. However, there is more to metacognition than just those four areas. There are also the areas of plan, monitor and evaluate (recognise these from somewhere?). Therefore, below are six new strategies (two planning, two monitoring and two evaluation) that will be developed in the same way as other strategies in this book, which you may wish to utilise during homework.

Exam Question Analysis
What

In this strategy, the focus is not on the actual answering of the question, but on analysing what the question is asking you to do. Therefore, there is no barrier for students regarding content for this strategy, as students do not have to be able to write up their answers to the question/task. Instead, students need to be able to provide some insight into what the task would be requiring them to do.

When/How

For the effective use of this strategy, you would need to select a question or task for students that requires a fair amount of time to comprehend. Too straightforward, and students' automatic response will be to simply answer the questions, whilst if the task is too complex to comprehend, it defeats the purpose of having a metacognitively focussed homework to avoid providing students with homework tasks that they cannot complete.

Despite saying in the first part of this strategy that students do not need to be able to answer the question, but simply make notes on what the question is asking them to do, including the content that is required in the answer, strategies that may be needed and potential methods for writing up the answer, it would still be unwise to provide students with a task where they are not confident with the content. Even if the purpose of the task is to comprehend the requirements, students will be put off with a question or task where they do not understand at all the content that it is covering.

This strategy is the perfect one to use in preparation for a lesson focusing on writing up extended answers. Students would be able to analyse one or more questions at home, and then come in to discuss tasks requirements further, before writing up their answer. This could be explored through teacher-led questioning, pair work or group work. One nice way to extend this activity would be to provide students with blank copies of the question again, and to have a 'master' copy of what the 'correct' comprehension may be.

Why

Often, we like to teach students the content required in class and get them to do the extended practice on the topic at home. This strategy flips this around, challenging students to consider and prepare for a task at home, and then potentially complete it in class (though you may decide that a simple evaluation of the question comprehension is sufficient). The main benefit of this is that, again, students do not need to be 100 per cent confident on content knowledge to be able to access this homework task. Instead, they just need to comprehend the question, making key notes on what they believe would need to be included and the way that they would go about completing the question. This homework task actually teaches students the need to take time to comprehend a question too, rather than just rushing straight in with an answer. By placing emphasis on analysis, you are showing students that they need to place an emphasis on this area, too.

Examples

I utilise exam question analysis as a superb homework task for my Year 11 GCSE students. One area that is crucial for GCSE mathematics students to improve in is their problem solving. These questions typically require a significant amount of comprehension as well as multiple lines of method, as students look to earn up to around 6 marks. However, I have found that students often have got the subject knowledge required to complete these questions, but not the know-how to complete these questions.

Therefore, I provide students with a range of problem-solving exam questions as homework. Their only task is to go through each of the questions, making notes on what the question is asking them to do, and how they would go about attempting the question. By using this strategy, there are three main bonuses. Firstly, students are spending their time improving their comprehension abilities, thus improving outcomes on problem-solving questions. Secondly, students are able to get through significantly more questions than if they were actually working them out. This means that students are making even more progress on their area of weakness. Lastly, students do not have the barrier of the maths to stop them from completing this homework. Regardless of their understanding of the topic, students can still note down their comprehension of the question and how they would go about answering it. Students do not even need to be on the right path to be able to do an exam question analysis task. So, overall, this strategy is a low-barrier, but high-impact way to use homework in your lessons.

Summary

- Provide students with an exam question. Students need to record notes on how they would approach the question, what content is included and how they would write up their answer.
- Here students do not need much, if any, subject knowledge, as they are just focusing on the comprehension of the given question. However, do not just choose a 'random' topic, as this may confuse students and lead to lower return rates/poor homework quality once again.
- The aim of this strategy is to emphasise the importance of planning and to support students' ability to comprehend exam questions.

Planning Document
What

This metacognitive strategy is one of the most subject specific of all of those presented within this book. The planning document strategy places an emphasis on students completing a planning document, as determined by yourself, for a given task. Here, there is no prescribed planning document. The planning document that you provide to students can be one that you use, one prescribed by your faculty or school, or even one recognised as the go-to planning strategy for your topic or subject area. Furthermore, the focus of this planning document is not on metacognition, but solely your subject-specific content. You do not need to change any planning document that you have already to make it more 'metacognitive'. Leave it as it is, as the metacognitive power comes later.

When/How

Much like with the previous strategy, the focus of the planning document strategy is not to challenge students on writing up an answer. However, as opposed to the previous strategy which did not place an emphasis on subject knowledge, this strategy does (as, of course, you are utilising one of your subject-specific planning documents).

However, once again, students are only planning to complete a task, again removing the barrier of poor subject knowledge. Yes, students are not going to be hugely successful using a planning document if they are not clear on the subject content, but they will be able to do something. If the task was to just write up the answer, then these students would probably do nothing at all.

These planning grids can be utilised once the subject knowledge has been taught, but not before. Equally, ensure that students are familiar with the planning grid. As this planning grid is one that you already use in your subject, this will hopefully not be an issue. Equally, because it is one that you use in your subject area, it will be one that you are more familiar and confident with, making this metacognitive strategy more straightforward than others to implement.

Why

Once again, the emphasis of this strategy is on removing the barrier of subject content. Though this strategy does require students to hold a fair amount of subject knowledge, all students should be able to record their plans to complete a task regardless of whether they are very confident or not overly confident, or have been present for all lessons, or have missed most lessons. However, the main aim again with this strategy is to place emphasis on planning (hence why it is a planning strategy). We know that planning is the first stage of one of the metacognitive cycles (and, actually, knowledge of self, knowledge of task and knowledge of strategies is all just planning too, really). Therefore, by providing students with this task, you are both emphasising the importance of planning to students, but you are also providing students with an explicit opportunity to improve their planning abilities, without having to worry about the actual task competition. By removing the task as a factor, students can instead focus their complete brain power on becoming the best planners possible.

Examples

Approaching extended writing tasks can be overwhelming when initially introduced to students. A scaffolded approach using a planning document is one way to guide students to produce well-structured, monitored pieces of work. Over continued use, students should internalise the questions addressed within the document – the scaffold being removed before key assessments to ensure independence.

The planning document can be divided into three sections: task knowledge, self-knowledge and strategy knowledge.

In the task knowledge column, students identify key components of the question such as the command word, key information, marks available and expectations regarding length of response. Explicitly highlighting this information guides their planning, making it clear that two sentences is insufficient to obtain 6 marks.

In the self-knowledge column, students write down key information which fits the parameters of the question. This could be terminology or definitions, formula, or processes. The information included within this section will form the bulk of their answer, so it is important that this information is well documented.

In the final column, strategy knowledge is included. This final section will vary most, based on task parameters and subject. It can include expansion on terminology or the organisation of information into an appropriate sequence. Additionally, it can be a checklist for key vocabulary that must be included, or similarities and differences for comparisons.

The planning document is versatile – being suitable for all departments irrespective of any acronyms used to support planning. In science BUG is used (Box the command word, Underline the key information and Generate a plan) whereas in English PEA is used (Point, Evidence, Analysis). The planning document complements both approaches, meaning use across a school can be easily embedded.

Whilst it is referred to as a planning document, this does encapsulate monitoring and reflection of successful task completion. The detailed plan produced can be used as a simple checklist for students to ensure that all relevant content is covered to track their progress.

When initially presented, and for continued use with lower KS3, it can be useful to pre-populate the document with key prompts such as strategies used to complete the question, as well as the information which needs to be gleaned from the question. Completion of a document should be modelled, making explicit the thought processes being used as it is filled out. Students will benefit from completing a document independently with a related, yet still distinct question. Prior activation of relevant knowledge during the modelling process will reduce cognitive load as students will not be attempting to navigate a new task whilst dedicating resources to retrieving information covered some time previously.

Question:		
Describe how a Leslie cube and other equipment could be used to compare how the type of surface affects the amount of infrared radiation emitted. Suggest any safety precautions. Your answer should include any steps necessary to reduce inaccuracies in the data [6 marks]		
Task Knowledge	**Self-knowledge**	**Strategy Knowledge**
• Command words • Key information • Marks available • Expectations	• Bullet point what you know • Topics required • Key words you need to use	• Key words to use • BUG approach • Sequence of information

Figure 9.1 One type of subject-specific planning grid that could be used

Rudi Carter

Summary

- Provide students with a planning grid that you already use within your subject.
- Students must complete the planning grid for a given task or question. Though students require subject knowledge to do this, it is not a barrier to at least attempting this question.
- The main aim of this strategy is to place a focus on planning, and provide students with an opportunity to work on this area explicitly.

Warning Signs

What

The warning signs strategy stems from the idea of metacognitive monitoring. Here, before completing a task, students will need to produce a list of warning signs. Warning signs are things that, should they appear within an answer, mean that the answer, or write-up, is most likely going in the correct direction. For example, if a History question on the events in the Second World War contained dates of events prior to 1939 and post-1945, alarm bells should be ringing.

When/How

This strategy is another superb one in supporting students' subject knowledge development. As students are focusing in on common misconceptions, and ensuring that they are not making them, they themselves are learning what the common misconceptions are, and how not to make them.

This strategy, due to its focus on misconceptions, would be a superb one to use after the metacognitive misconceptions discussion strategy detailed earlier in the book. Students could work together, or be teacher led, in developing a list of common misconceptions around the topic area that they had just studied. Students could then take this list with them as their 'warning signs' scaffold, and utilise this to support the monitoring of their homework task. This is one way where there can be joined up thinking between two or more different metacognitive strategies, and ensuring that in-class and out-of-class work is more seamless and builds off each other.

Why

Monitoring is such a crucial area in life, generally. Without getting into too many details, monitoring is the ability to ensure that you are heading in the correct direction in the task that you are completing. This may be in regard to time, or more specifically in regards to the content that is required in an answer to meet the task criteria. However, for numerous different reasons, humans are not very good at monitoring. Once we have invested time and effort in one direction, it is human nature to keep following this path, even if it were quicker to start again and go off in a different direction.

To be successful in task competition, then, we need to know when we are going wrong. Otherwise, even if we are attempting to monitor our task progress, if we do not know what we are looking for, we will still only be able to evaluate task success once we have completed the overall task. This may be too late then to make any corrections needed. By producing a 'warning signs' list of common misconceptions that, should they appear in our answer, we know we are heading in the wrong direction, and need to pause and re-consider our approach, students are going to be in a far better position to make changes before it is too late. Equally, the more frustration that we can save students (of investing time and energy only to find out they are 'wrong' at the end), the better. We do not want students to think that their time and effort has been wasted.

Examples

When I decide to focus on exam technique with A-level pupils, I am a big fan of working on 'Do's' and 'Don'ts' together. I will typically begin a lesson with that as the Do Now. For my Year 12s who are now 8 months into the course, I will pose a scenario: You are meeting a Year 12 who has just begun the course; write a list of 'Do's' and 'Don'ts' for them to help them tackle 6-mark analyse questions. Pupils then produce a long list of these and we come together and do a class discussion, adding them all to my list on the whiteboard. We discuss them and I ensure they know the 'why': Why exactly is X not something we should be doing? This part is key – if not done, this lesson becomes something easily forgettable, but when you add in their own justification it becomes really memorable for them moving forward.

I will have printed mark schemes, one part of our evidence base, which they use to add evidence; that is, specific quotes from mark schemes which back up a 'Don't'. The other source of evidence are snippets from examiner reports, which I have pre-selected and which we discuss, to add yet more justification for why certain aspects are 'Don'ts'. Finally, I present them with a 6-mark analysis question and they put their advice to the test!

Alternatively, I may pose this question for my Year 13s: 'What makes a bad 20-mark essay?' Again, pupils write their ideas, with the focus this time being purely 'negative'; that is, I don't ask, 'What makes a good 20-mark essay?' The same discussion as above follows and we end by either planning or writing a response to a 20-marker.

Abdurrahman Pérez-McMillan

Summary

- Ensure that students have a list of common misconceptions for the topic area that is being questioned by the given homework task.
- This list could be developed through a teacher- or group-led discussion in the lesson before the homework is given.

- The purpose of monitoring is to ensure that the task is being successfully completed, and to spot mistakes and required changes in approach as soon as possible.

Flow Maps
What

A flow map is another one of those amazing graphic organisers. A flow map, as the name begins to suggests, is a sequencing graphic organiser, where the stages of an event or the chronology of events are recorded. However, as a metacognitive strategy, the flow map is used to record the stages that a student would need to work through in order to complete a task. In this specific scenario, students would record the stages required to complete a given homework task.

When/How

This specific strategy could be used for all homework tasks, really. It does not need to be something that takes a long time, and it also does not need to be something that is always student led. For example, you could just provide students with a flow map that you have created for a specific task (possibly on the reverse of a homework sheet), and then students could utilise this. Doing it this way would save a significant amount of time within a lesson (even cutting it to zero if you always provide a flow map for students). Alternatively, you could spend five minutes towards the end of a lesson going through the homework task with students, and cold calling around to get the stages needed for a flow map for that homework task. Equally, you may have already developed a flow map for at the start of a topic to support with in-class work, so students may just need to take their books home.

One point to be cautious about with the flow map is it is meant as a reminder for students on the stages that they are going through. It should not be used by students as an automatic process where they are moving through these stages without even thinking. Instead, the purpose is to ensure that students are staying on task and working towards a successful conclusion.

Why

As with the previous strategy, the focus with this strategy is on monitoring – ensuring that students are successfully working through a task towards a positive outcome. One of the main benefits of this strategy is the removal of cognitive load. When completing a task, it is often difficult to recall all of the correct steps, all in the correct order, whilst also working with complex and newly learnt subject content. Therefore, by producing a flow map, we are removing this cognitive load, thus making it easier for students to focus on the subject content. By having this checklist of steps to work through, we are providing the scaffold that our students require to work through a task or problem in a logical order, once more helping to ensure that effort and time is spent wisely.

Examples

Flow map for evaluating an exam

Feedback on an assessment is crucial for moving learning forward. However, it is important that students are actively engaging with the feedback in a way which helps them build a better understanding of their own strengths and weaknesses. Flow maps can be used to help students when reflecting on their exam performance. The example below would be used alongside teacher modelling to explicitly show how they should approach moving their learning forward when they have lost marks on a question. This resource is designed to explicitly demonstrate the thought processes that they need to follow when evaluating their performance and it is done in a way which is easy to follow. In the classroom, this resource would be modelled by the teacher, showing the students how to use it whilst also explaining why each part of the process is important. Initially this would be a resource which is used every time evaluation needs to take place, but over time the process will become more autonomous and develop into the way pupils naturally approach reflecting on their performance.

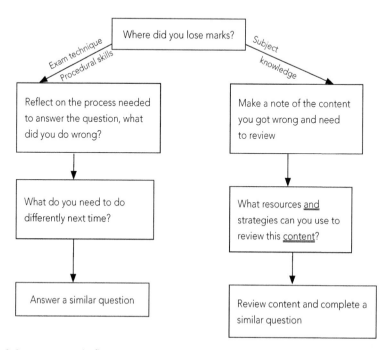

Figure 9.2 An example flow map, used to support students' self-evaluation

Lauren Stephenson

Summary

- Either produce or work with students to produce a flow map (i.e. step-by-step guide) of the stages required to complete a task.
- Students refer to the flow map to ensure that they are working through the stages in the correct order.
- Ensure that students are using the scaffold as a monitoring strategy, rather than a copy and repeat but with different numbers/words scaffold.

Wrappers

What

A wrapper is perhaps one of the more commonly used strategies in this book, used in particular with exam classes in a range of different subjects. Though it is perhaps a strategy that you have used, or may currently be using, it is still worth considering the metacognitive value of a wrapper. This in turn may refine and improve your own teaching practice yet further.

A wrapper is a strategy to support evaluation, and is typically provided to students following an assessment or mock exam. This wrapper can be broken down into many different parts, but often focusses on at least three areas. The first is pre-assessment/pre-mock preparation. How did the student prepare for that assessment? How long did they spend preparing? The second stage often focusses on the assessment/mock itself, sometimes with a question-by-question breakdown. Here, students will be considering where they dropped marks, and self-evaluating the reasons for this. In the final part of the wrapper, students will consider what changes they will make moving forward in order to improve outcomes at their next assessment or mock.

When/How

As mentioned above, a wrapper will be given to students typically after a mock or assessment. However, there will be times where it could be given after a more significant homework task, or possibly after some in-class learning.

The wrapper is also an extremely versatile tool. So long as the main premise of the wrapper is to provide students with the required directed scaffold to support their own evaluation, and so long as there are sections on before the task and after, then the foci of the questions can be varied. You may need to change them depending on the group that you are working with, or depending upon the subject that you teach. Many of the questions detailed within a wrapper will also be questions that you are already asking students. Therefore, it is just a process of bringing them all together to form the wrapper that you want. An example is shown below that might give you inspiration for your own.

Why

Though we want students to be evaluating constantly, question-by-question, task-by-task, lesson-by-lesson, if we are ever going to have students evaluating, that must be after an assessment or mock. These are the points where students will hopefully have completed substantial amounts of revision and will hopefully have given a good account of themselves and their subject knowledge. This wrapper, therefore, allows for effective evaluation of why this may, or may not, have been the case, as well as strengths, weaknesses and alternative approaches for future assessments/mocks.

Furthermore, a wrapper allows for formal evaluation. This means that students will have a record of their evaluation. In fact, an A3 wrapper sheet can literally wrap around a mock exam paper (hence the name of wrapper). This will allow students to monitor their progress over time (or wrapper by wrapper), which is not something that could necessarily be done if evaluation was conducted in an alternative way – such as with evaluative questioning or 'two stars and a wish'.

Examples

Students' first concern when receiving an assessment back is the number of marks attained, shortly followed by what grade said score translates into. Whilst a focus on a score cannot be removed, this rarely leads to meaningful reflection. Following assessments, students complete an exam wrapper which guides them to reflect on preparation, performance, and what to change next time. It is important that students are explicitly told to be honest at each stage, as this is the only way to make the process effective.

The entire process relies on clear modelling. It is useful to have an example of an examiner's report and student response, or a pre-written 'student' response. With this you can then model to students how to identify missed marks and complete the wrapper appropriately.

Before students receive their papers, they complete the pre-assessment section which details their revision strategies. Within this they state how many hours they (approximately) spent revising, as well as providing a breakdown by technique (flash cards, reading notes, watching videos, etc.). It has been beneficial to do this beforehand so that students do not alter the time spent to reflect their performance – I didn't do well, so therefore will say I didn't revise to save face.

Once students receive their papers, they are given time to review their performance. During this time, they are guided to choose a question they performed best on, and the question which they struggled with. Their strength or strengths are identified, and the skills which they demonstrated are explicitly discussed. It is critical that the exam wrapper does not become a focus purely on the lost marks. Students need also to reflect on what they did well, and the linked techniques. It may be that they performed well on a question about ionic bonding because they focussed on past exam questions to identify mark expectations but performed less well on questions where their strategy was to passively read notes.

When considering targets, students are guided to consider where marks were lost, using both assessment objective criteria and question expectations. They approximate lost marks based on A01, A02, A03 criteria, unclear question expectations and lack of knowledge to produce a response. These criteria circumvent responses such as 'I didn't know the answer', pushing students to consider what they need to focus on moving ahead. Time permitting, the process can be repeated for other questions so that patterns can be identified.

The final, and most critical, step to drive progress is planning for future revision strategies. Students are asked to consider three things that they will do differently when preparing for future assessments. Some scaffolding may be needed at this stage, again guided by class discussion and modelling. Within this final stage students need to consider where they currently are, where they want to be and how they are going to get there. Do they need to be more active with their revision, practise approaches to questions on the same topic with differing command words, or do they need to ensure appropriate time is dedicated to preparation? A section is also provided for students to detail the support they want from their teacher moving ahead. Although as practitioners we can reflect on the skills they need support with following marking, this question often elucidates gaps in knowledge of appropriate strategies to use which can then be actively built into a lesson.

Post-assessment reflection

This is an opportunity for you to reflect on your assessment performance, and more importantly reflect on the effectiveness of your exam preparation. Answer these questions honestly, as only true reflection and future planning will allow us to determine how to best support your learning.

1 Approximately how much time did you spend preparing for this assessment?
2 How did you prepare yourself for the assessment? Identify which of the methods you used, and the approximate time spent on each strategy.

   a   Reviewing your notes

   b   Using your revision book

   c   Producing and using flash cards

   d   Answering practice exam questions

   e   Watching videos online

   f   Other (please specify)

3 Identifying strengths. Review the question where you performed best (% of marks rather than absolute marks). Why did you perform well on this question?

Consider: use of key vocabulary, understanding of the command word, use of key definitions, clear expression of knowledge.

4   Identifying targets. Review the question where you lost the most marks.

What was the question out of? _____   How many marks did you gain? _____

Reflect on why you lost marks – this is the best way to make future progress as you can identify skills to develop.

Approximate the marks you lost due to:

a   Trouble demonstrating knowledge and understanding of scientific ideas, scientific techniques and procedures (A01)

b   Trouble applying knowledge and understanding of scientific ideas, scientific enquiry, techniques and procedures (A02)

c   Trouble analysing information and ideas to interpret and evaluate, make judgements and draw conclusions (A03)

d   Unclear expectations of the question

e   Not knowing how to approach the question

f   Other (specify)

5   Based on your responses to the information above **state at least three things you will do differently in preparing for the next assessment**; for example, spend more time comparing your knowledge with the specification to ensure that you can approach questions proposed.

6   What can I do to support your learning and preparation for future assessments?

Figure 9.3   A possible approach to supporting structured student self-evaluation and future planning

Rudi Carter

Summary

- Produce a wrapper, containing evaluative questions on the preparation for the assessment, evaluation of the assessment questions, and questions on future approaches.

- Keep these formal directed points of evaluation so that students can track their progress over time.
- Adapt your wrappers to suit your subject content and the classes that you teach.

PMI Grid

What

Where the wrapper strategy is a lengthier form of evaluation, the PMI grid is a straightforward and time-saving strategy to support student evaluation. PMI (or plus, minus, interesting) is a templated evaluation document that students can complete following a series of lessons or the completion of a topic. In addition, a final stage of 'aims' can be added. This allows students to complete further reflection to consider where they might move to next.

When/How

As mentioned above, the PMI grid is likely to be used after a series of lessons or a topic. However, there are places where it could be used after just one lesson, as a plenary or exit activity. The simplicity of the PMI grid also means that multiple blank templates can be printed out and stored in a cupboard, ready to use at a moment's notice.

Furthermore, the PMI grid is highly simplistic, and therefore is an evaluative model that, once modelled to students on one occasion, should be something that they can complete on all occasions. This therefore means that it could be a potential homework task. Where students have completed a unit, that evening may provide a chance for students to complete a PMI, perhaps ready to discuss it within a group in their next lesson.

Why

Evaluation is something that we need students to be doing all of the time. This is where the PMI grid comes into its own. Due to the simplicity of the grid, and the ability to have blank templates ready to go at the drop of a hat, the PMI grid provides us with a go-to option to support student evaluation. It is true that it may not be the most in-depth evaluative strategy, or even the most specific strategy, either. However, it is not always possible to develop a highly thought-out set of evaluative questions or to put together a wrapper. Therefore, we need straightforward and effective strategies that do support student evaluation. The PMI grid is just that.

Examples

The PMI grid makes a fantastic summary homework for PHSE lessons. As PHSE lessons are more infrequent, students require a shorter homework task, which makes the PMI grid suitable. Equally, with PHSE lessons being few and far between, the PMI grid provides a log of student reflections, which allows for students to keep a track of their learning through collecting together their PMI grids.

To ensure that students were happy completing the PMI grid at home, students first completed several PMI grids at the end of lessons to ensure that they were clear on what they needed to do, and were confident with doing this. Also, clear explanations of how to complete a PMI grid were placed on our online homework board, so that parents were able to support students as and where required.

Overall, the PMI grid provided an easy-to-complete homework for students that ensured consistent reflection, as well as a collective of reflections over the course of a half-term or so.

Summary

- A PMI stands for: plus, minus, interesting.
- A section on future aims/improvements can also be added to the structure.
- This is a less specific and in-depth evaluative strategy, but is a template that we can quickly go to with very low barriers of entry for students.

Summary

- Homework is a consistent expectation of teachers – so if we are going to set it, we may as well make it as good as it can be!
- Students often struggle to complete homework due to poor recall of content. Metacognitive approaches to homework help to lessen this barrier.
- A range of new planning, monitor and evaluation homework ideas have been presented, which may make suitable homework alternatives.

Further Reading

The following readings provide a greater insight into what makes effective homework:

Dabell, J. (2019). 'Research Analysis: Getting the Most Out of Homework', SecEd, available at: www.sec-ed.co.uk/best-practice/research-analysis-getting-the-most-out-of-homework/ (accessed 7 May 2022)

EEF (2021). 'Homework', Education Endowment Foundation, available at: https://educationendowmentfoundation.org.uk/education-evidence/teaching-learning-toolkit/homework (accessed 7 May 2022)

Enser, M. (2019). '5 Rules to Make Homework Worth Their Time (and Yours), Tes, available at: www.tes.com/magazine/archive/5-rules-make-homework-worth-their-time-and-yours (accessed 7 May 2022)

Jones, A. (2021). 'Seven Principles of Effective Secondary Homework', SecEd, available at: www.sec-ed.co.uk/best-practice/seven-principles-of-effective-secondary-homework-school-education-home-curriculum-learning-homework-with-impact-routledge/ (accessed 7 May 2022)

Here are some further details on other metacognitive strategies:

Burns, N. (2021). 'Metacognition: 7 Strategies to Use in Any Class', *Tes*, available at: www.tes.com/magazine/archived/metacognition-7-strategies-use-any-class (accessed 7 May 2022)

10
Online Learning

Learning Objectives

In this chapter we will:

- Consider the implication on metacognition when teaching remotely
- Review approaches to remote teaching and learning to support the greatest metacognitive development in our students as possible

Introduction

As with the last chapter, these next few pages are going to consider metacognition outside of the physical classroom. The purpose of this chapter will be to consider remote teaching. Four areas of remote teaching practice will be considered, in order to evaluate the best way to support metacognitive development in students.

Online Learning

By the time you are reading this book, hopefully online-only learning will be something that is recent history. As a profession, we found a way not just to deliver teaching to our students during a global pandemic, but we also found extremely high-quality ways to do that, and ensured as much learning as possible was taking place. Despite the successes of this, and the strides made in remote schooling, in-person teaching is of course what we want to be doing moving forward. However, there are some lessons that we can learn for any virtual teaching that we might do in the future. Maybe this will be for some online tutoring, or the end of the snow day when all teaching moves online with only an hour's notice.

Focus on skills rather than content

One of the most difficult aspects of online learning was clear communication with students. How often would the Internet lag, or a couple of students ask questions or make points at exactly the same time? As with any online video, there is always some sort of issue. Therefore, pushing on through new content can be extremely difficult. Whether there be a lag, a sudden noise, crackling or something else, students listening can very quickly lose track of what is being said, and hence struggle to pick up on the new learning. If these issues continue over a number of lessons, you could find yourself with several students who are completely lost, despite being confident that your delivery and teaching had been good. The alternative, therefore, is to spend time focusing on strategies for content that students are already confident with. If the worst comes to the worst, and students are not following this teaching, at least they are not falling behind on content.

So, what would this look like? Rather than ploughing through new content, consider what you have recently taught to students, probably face-to-face, and are confident that they understand. Once this knowledge block has been determined, consider the different cognitive strategies that students need to employ to be success. Also, spend time considering key misconceptions and points of learning, which would help to inform metacognitive development. This information will allow you to select suitable metacognitive strategies to use within your online lessons. For example, you could spend time discussing the different strategies available to tackle a problem based upon recently taught content. Why not re-attempt the same questions, but with different strategies to stimulate discussion over the utility of different strategies? The options here are fairly limitless, and as long as the focus is on metacognitive development based upon previous learnt knowledge, you will not be going too far wrong.

Consider how to question effectively and develop discussion

The most difficult part of remote teaching is assessment of student understanding. Gone is your ability to quickly cold call, or get students to show their physical whiteboard. Instead, alternative strategies or workarounds are needed in order to assess students understanding. This of course can hit metacognitive development quite hard. Questioning and discussion is a huge part of the teacher toolkit – so how can these be amended to suit remote teaching?

Fortunately, there are a huge amount of tech-savvy individuals out there, who wrote extensively during the main UK lockdown about technologies which could be used to support these key areas of teaching. More ideas and readings can be found at the end of this chapter, but here are some key ideas:

- Breakout rooms – these allow you to place a small number of students into their own video call, where they can personally discuss a certain topic area. Time limits can be set and, once completed, students can all return to the main lesson to continue on. This strategy allows you to place students of your choice into groups, much as you would do within a lesson. Again, much like in-person teaching, you can go from breakout room to breakout room, allowing you to monitor the progress of all of your students.

- Chat-box questions – one option is to provide written answers within the chat box of whichever video service you are using. Students can then like or respond to these comments, giving you instant evaluation of student understanding. It would also be a useful tool to evaluate which strategies students were using overall – crucial information for a conversation on strategy utility.
- Virtual whiteboards – there are now numerous online ways for students to be able to work on a whiteboard on their screen, and for you to see all of these whiteboards simultaneously, and draw up different ones to have a look in greater detail. This potentially has a greater benefit than whiteboards in person, as students are unable to copy when they cannot see each other's boards.
- Polls – much like using likes on a comment, it is also possible to set up polls for students to respond to. This is probably an easier method for longer-worded answers, and also opens up the option for students to leave written feedback and comments that you can utilise to inform your teaching, too. Depending on the platform that you are using, it may be possible to set up these polls within the main lesson or chat box, or it may be that you need to use alternative technologies, such as Show My Homework or Kahoot. Either way, these quick-fire polls and quizzes are a superb way for both you and students to evaluate their understanding with the content covered so far.

Modelling

Online learning is all about the modelling. Yes we can question, yes we can use polls, or breakout rooms and online whiteboards, but the most consistent learning will be your modelling to students. We also need to consider that students may just be viewing this on a phone screen too. So a small screen, and a potentially poor connection, we are up against it, which is where high-quality modelling comes up trumps.

It is rather fortunate, therefore, that there is a full chapter on metacognitively modelling at the start of this book. It is also fortunate too, that each of these strategies can be adapted and utilised for online teaching, especially the use of a visualiser. A visualiser is probably the go-to method of modelling while online teaching, where the use of your whiteboard is just not possible. However, each of the alternative strategies mentioned can also be utilised, again under the visualiser, to develop the type of metacognitive thinking that you want to be working on with your class.

Structured questions/directed learning

Remote teaching provides a good opportunity to get students to spend more time evaluating their learning. With students having significantly less scaffolding and support when they are working remotely, students are more reliant on their own skills and strategies. Yet, students of course are not typically good self-evaluators (who is until they are 'forced' to start doing it?). Therefore, online learning provides the perfect opportunity to start supporting students in self-evaluation of their learning. Of course, students are going to be able to do this without support, and so two alternative approaches can be used. The first is through structured questions, and the second is through directed learning.

Structured questioning is a strategy that revolves around providing students with a set of questions which they need to answer in order to evaluate their work or strategies that they have been using. There are numerous questions that could be asked, and so it would be up to you to identify the most suitable questions for the task just completed and the student(s) that you are working with.

Examples of questions that could be used include:

- Did you meet all of the objectives for the task? How do you know?
- What are the main strengths of your answer? How do you know?
- What are your areas for improvement now, and how are you going to address these?
- How would you plan for this task if you were to do it again?
- What would you keep the same and what would you change about your approach to this task if you were going to do it again?
- What information were you lacking in the task?
- What support or scaffold could help complete this task better, and why do you think this?
- Did the strategy you chose work as expected?
- Would you use the same strategy again if you were to complete this task once more?
- Can you see when the strategy you just used may not be appropriate to use?
- What makes the strategy you chose more effective than others for this activity?

As with any of these metacognitive strategies, students are going to need to be trained on using the strategy effectively and correctly. Therefore, before providing students with these questions, it would be wise to model two or three of these questions to students first. This might involve you writing our full answers and talking through your thinking, or it may just involve you simply talking through key things to consider. It may also be worth considering providing students with additional scaffolds the first time that they use the questions. Rather than just providing students with the questions and hoping that they are listening and can accurately recall the points that you told them to write about, you could provide brief bullet points with each question detailing the content that they need to cover. This provides students with a reference that they can refer back to in order to answer these questions to the best of their abilities.

The second strategy that can be utilised is directed learning. Though similar to the strategy above, directed learning instead provides tasks to students in order to support the evaluation of their work. This could come in numerous formats, but could include:

- redoing the task again but using an alternative strategy;
- providing a student with a scaffold, such as a Knowledge Organiser, to allow students to add in further details and make corrections as required;

- comparing their answer against a high-quality, pre-marked and pre-graded answer, to allow the student to compare and contrast the features that they included in their answers;
- providing students with a mark scheme to allow them to consider where marks would be awarded for the task they were completing, and therefore what features did they include and what features do they need to include next time.

To further improve the benefits from this evaluation, students could then receive a follow-up task that assesses similar skills and requires similar strategies (as opposed to content) and allow students to apply their new learning to produce a superior answer than they did the first time around. Evaluation is of course a hugely beneficial tool, but without the opportunity to apply this learning to new tasks and cement changes in long-term approaches, the new learning that students will have made will very quickly be forgotten, and the same mistakes will be made over and over again.

Summary

- When teaching remotely, all metacognitive approaches will need to be reconsidered to ensure they remain appropriate for the teaching setting.
- It is worth spending greater time on skills rather than content where there are communication difficulties.
- Utilise chat functions and breakout rooms to allow metacognitive questioning and discussion to continue.

Further Reading

These readings provide high-quality guidance on remote teaching:

Dartmouth College (2022). 'Teach Remotely – How to Teach From Anywhere', *Dartmouth College*, available at: https://sites.dartmouth.edu/teachremote/remote-teaching-good-practices/ (accessed 07 May 2022)

EEF (2020). 'Remote Learning – Rapid Evidence Review', Education Endowment Foundation, available at: https://educationendowmentfoundation.org.uk/public/files/Publications/Covid-19_Resources/Remote_learning_evidence_review/Remote_Learning_Rapid_Evidence_Assessment.pdf (accessed 7 May 2022)

Enser, M. (2021). 'Remote Learning: How to Apply Rosenshine's Principles', *TES*, available at: https://www.tes.com/magazine/archived/remote-learning-how-apply-rosenshines-principles (accessed 07 May 2022)

Lough, C. (2021). 'How to Do Remote Learning "Well": Ofsted's 7 Top Tips', *Tes*, available at: www.tes.com/magazine/archived/how-do-remote-learning-well-ofsteds-7-top-tips (accessed 7 May 2022)

11
Key Takeaways

Learning Objectives

In this chapter we will:

- Review the key points made in each chapter
- Provide a summary of the metacognitive strategies that you can use in your classroom
- Provide a one chapter 'pit-stop' for all of your metacognitive revision.

Introduction

One thing that I believe educational books are often missing are summaries. You may have read through the 200-odd pages scrupulously, but this does not mean that you can remember all of the amazing things that were covered in the book. Hopefully, this book is exactly the same! However, to prevent you from having to go right back through this book to find the bullet point or strategy that you really need to find out about in the two minutes that you have, this book instead has a very handy, one-chapter review of all of the key points of the book. Enjoy!

Metacognition – What It Is and Why It Matters

Metacognition has a very long history, having been around for at least a half-century in the mainstream of educational theory. Developed by Brown, Schraw and Flavell, metacognition is not self-regulation (but is rather part of the umbrella of self-regulation). Flavell provides a key definition for the understanding of what metacognition is:

> I am being metacognitive if I notice that I am having more trouble learning A than B; if it strikes me that I should double check C before accepting it as fact.

I also attempt to define metacognition, as:

> The little voice inside you head that constantly evaluates and informs your actions.

Metacognition itself can be broken down into knowledge of cognition (understanding our own areas of cognition) and regulation of cognition (how we control and monitor our thinking).

Knowledge of cognition is broken down into:

- *Knowledge of self* – the cognition we can draw upon in a task.
- *Knowledge of strategies* – the approaches we have for a task.
- *Knowledge of task* – the comprehension of the task.

Regulation of cognition is broken down into:

- *Planning* – the preparation prior to attempting a task.
- *Monitoring* – the ongoing monitoring to ensure that the task is heading in the correct direction.
- *Evaluation* – a consideration of strengths and weaknesses of the approach taken and the outcome.

It was concluded that metacognitive skills do not translate successfully from one subject to another, and potentially even from one topic to another within a subject domain. This is because the 'meta' is in relation to the 'cognition', and therefore where cognition varies, so does the meta. Though it would be unwise to presume that metacognitive skills does translate from one area to another, if students have got strong knowledge of metacognitive strategies (such as how to evaluate their work), these skills should still translate fairly well across domains.

The rationale provided for metacognition is significant. The EEF detail metacognition as the most impactful new intervention that can be introduced within schools. Ofsted also suggest that metacognition is a powerful strategy that a successful staff-CPD programme would include. Above and beyond that, vast swathes of research prove that metacognition is a highly impactful strategy that should be implemented across all subjects within secondary schools.

Metacognitive Myths

There are four common (or at least, far too common!) myths surrounding metacognition. These four myths are:

1   Metacognition is only for the most able.
2   Metacognition is not for SEN students.

3   Metacognition is only for older students.
4   Metacognition is only for girls.

All four of these are myths. Where they have developed from is unclear, but much is probably to do with complex nature of metacognitive theory, making individuals believe that metacognition can only be for those who achieve highly and have great understanding of their subject areas. However, the rationale for metacognition shows that developing metacognition is suitable for all students. Metacognition is explicitly linked to cognition, which is something we *all* utilise daily. Therefore, if it is something that we are all doing almost every minute of every day, then we ought to be developing it in our students.

Metacognitive Strategies

A range of different strategies, covering metacognitive processes, modelling, questioning and discussion were all considered. There are strategies available to suit all students, all year groups and every subject going.

Successful implementation

The key areas to consider as an individual implementing metacognitive strategies are:

1   Revise

       Ensure that you are thoroughly confident with metacognitive theory before you begin to implement. The more confident (and clearer) you are, the better your implementation will be.

2   Choose a suitable class

       Make sure that you choose a class who display positive behaviour, and have a fair amount of resilience. This will buy you some time and space to make mistakes and experiment without concern over behavioural difficulties.

3   Consider what the weaknesses are

       Once you have decided on a class, ensure that you identify a specific area that you want that class to improve on, and a clear strategy that will improve that area. Do not choose a strategy before you decide on the area that a class needs to work on.

4   Have your resources ready

       Do not leave your preparation to the break before you first use the strategy. Make sure to have everything prepared well in advance, including any scripting that you need to do.

5   Script your lines

Whether you are an early careers teacher, or have years of teaching under your belt, scripting key phrases that you will use when introducing your new metacognitive strategy will be extremely helpful. These scripted lines will ensure that you are being clear, concise and accurate in what you are saying.

6   Short-term planning

Make sure that you schedule in a suitable point to utilise your strategy. Make sure as well, that this will be a point in the unit where students have sufficient clarity on content and alternative strategies, as without this students will be focusing too much on the subject content rather than their metacognitive thinking.

7   Long-term planning

Make sure that you plan multiple opportunities into your learning sequence where you can re-use the same metacognitive strategy. Without this, you will not have the opportunity to act upon reflections and make improvements, and students will not have the required practice to thoroughly understand the strategy and make the desired metacognitive improvements.

8   Get some feedback

Where possible, get a trusted colleague to come and observe you using your new shiny strategy. It does not matter if this colleague is a metacognitive expert or not, as you will be able to share with them the strategy you are using, and the aim of using this strategy. Utilise their feedback when you do your own evaluation of how successful your implementation was.

9   Compare to your aims

Make sure that you pencil in time to reflect on the use of your new strategy. Compare what happened to your aims of the strategy. Consider your own delivery, and how confident you are (and what evidence you have) to suggest that you were successful (or, unsuccessful). Consider what you will do differently next time that you use the strategy so that you are more successful.

10   Take your time

Do not put too much pressure on yourself. Give these strategies a go, continue to reflect and do not stress if it does not go to plan!

The key areas to consider as a department or school-wide leader, if you are wanting to introduce metacognitive strategies on a wider scale, are:

1   Identify the main weakness

As a class teacher would identify a weakness for a specific class, you will need to identify a weakness for a particular department, year group or whole school.

Ensure that you are clear on this weakness and evidence that this is the most crucial area to work on. Make sure that you then identify up to three strategies that you want staff to implement at any one time.

2   Training needs

Consider how you are going to ensure staff are skilled up in metacognitive theory and strategies. Will you deliver CPD to staff? Will you buy each a copy of this book? Will you just hope for the best?

3   Ensure consistency

You will need to ensure that all staff are implementing strategies in the same way. To support with this, identify key features of each strategy that you would expect to see each staff member displaying in your classroom. Make these key criteria obvious, so that all staff know what they should be doing, and what they should be seeing.

4   Do not rush

Do not try to implement these new strategies too quickly. Three new strategies will probably take one complete term to introduce, practise, refine and embed correctly. If you push to do it quicker, you will not have sustained success over the long term. Produce a timeframe so that you know what you should be seeing at each stage of your department/school journey.

5   Do not stop there

Once you have cemented those first few strategies, continue to implement new strategies, following the first four points above. Ensure that teaching gets better, and outcomes continue to improve. Become that metacognitive school!

Metacognitive Homework

Homework is something that, whether we support it or we do not, we typically need to set for each of our classes on a weekly basis. However, we will all struggle with similar issues, including poor-quality, low-return rates and excuses, particularly around forgetting how to do things. Therefore, several suggestions were made to support the development of metacognitive homework:

1   Place a focus on metacognitive processes rather than content. Students can struggle to recall content required for standard homework tasks, and so students can complete metacognitive tasks without the subject knowledge requirements.

2   Consider appropriate scaffolds that could be given to students to support them when completing homework. This may include process graphics, providing problem-solving grids or written reminders over good working environments.

3   Alternative metacognitive strategies, focusing on planning, monitoring and evaluation can also be considered.

Online Learning

Having spent many months mastering remote teaching during the COVID-19 pandemic, it is worth considering how metacognitive practices can be amended to suit such remote learning. These points are summarised below:

1   Place a focus on skills rather than content. With buffering and connection difficulties, students may be missing new content. However, by placing a focus on metacognitive considerations of recently learnt (in-person) content, students can continue to learn without fear of missing out on new subject-specific knowledge.

2   Consider a range of different questioning techniques, such as virtually hands up, breakout rooms and polls, to ensure that metacognitive questions and assessment for learning can still happen effectively.

3   Continue to take time to consider the most appropriate form of modelling, as this is even more crucial when students are just focusing on a small computer screen.

4   Provide students with structured questions which students work through to ensure that they evaluate the work and/or strategies that they have been using. Consider as well how to use directed learning, where students complete additional tasks to support their evaluation, such as redoing a task again but using an alternative strategy.

References

Artzz, A. F. and Armour-Thomas, E. (1992). 'Development of a Cognitive-Metacognitive Framework for Protocol Analysis of Mathematical Problem Solving in Small Groups', *Cognition and Instruction*, 9 (2), pp. 137–175.

Barton, C. (2020). *Reflect, Expect, Check, Explain: Sequences and Behaviour to Enable Mathematical Thinking in the Classroom*. Woodbridge: John Catt.

Ben-David, A. and Zohar, A. (2009). 'Contribution of Meta-Strategic Knowledge to Scientific Inquiry Learning', *International Journal of Science Education*, 31 (12), pp. 1657–1682.

Berger, R. (2003). *An Ethic of Excellence: Building a Culture of Craftsmanship with Students*. Portsmouth: Heinemann.

Brown, A. L. and DeLoache, J. S. (1978). 'Skills, Plans and Self-Regulation'. In R. S. Siegler (ed.), *Children's Thinking: What Develops?* Hillsdale, NJ: Lawrence Erlbaum Associates.

Callan, G., Marchant, G., Finch, H. and German, R. (2016). 'Metacognition, Strategies, Achievement, and Demographics: Relationships across Countries', *Educational Sciences: Theory and Practice*, October, pp. 1485–1504.

Caviglioli, O. (2019). *Dual Coding with Teachers*. Woodbridge: John Catt.

Davies, S. (2020). *Talking about Oracy*. Woodbridge: John Catt.

Demie, F. and Lewis, K. (2011). 'White Working Class Achievement: An Ethnographic Study of Barriers to Learning in Schools', *Educational Studies*, 37 (3), pp. 245–264.

Didau, D. (2019). *Making Kids Cleverer: A Manifesto for Closing the Advantage Gap*. Carmarthen: Crown House Publishing Limited.

Education Endowment Foundation (2018). 'Metacognition and Self-Regulated Learning: Guidance Report', *EEF*, pp. 1–32.

Education Endowment Foundation (2021). *Putting Evidence to Work: A School's Guide to Implementation*, EEF, pp. 1–48.

Ellis, A. K., Denton, D. W. and Bond, J. B. (2014). 'An Analysis of Research on Metacognitive Teaching Strategies', *Procedia-Social and Behavioral Sciences*, 116, pp. 4015–4024.

Enser, Z. and Enser, M. (2020). *Fiorella & Mayer's Generative Learning in Action*, John Catt Educational.

Flavell, J. H. (1976). 'Metacognitive Aspects of Problem Solving'. In L. B. Resnick (ed.), *The Nature of Intelligence* (pp. 231–235). Hillsdale, NJ: Lawrence Erlbaum.

Flavell, J. H., Miller, P. H. and Miller, S. A. (2002). *Cognitive Development* (4th edn). Upper Saddle River, NJ: Pearson Education Inc.

Gorski, P. C. (2016). 'Poverty and the Ideological Imperative: A Call to Unhook from Deficit and Grit Ideology and to Strive for Structural Ideology', *Teacher Education. Journal of Education for Teaching*, 42 (4), pp. 378–386.

Hattie, J. (2012). *Visible Learning for Teachers: Maximising Impact on Learning*. New York: Routledge.

Jones, J. (2015). 'Mathematics Mastery Primary Conference', available at: http://toolkit. mathematicsmastery.org/app/webroot/js/tiny_mce/plugins/moxiemanager/data/files/ Ofsted.pdf (accessed 18 April 2022).

Kettlewell, J. (2020). 'Working with Parents to Help Support the Development of Metacognition', Researchschool.org, available at: https://researchschool.org.uk/ news/working-with-parents-to-help-support-the-development-of-metacognition/ yu1Y1iIscWbqw2ERuxwDEpp2iGTARVwF/ (accessed 10 March 2020).

Kirschner, P. and Hendrick, C. (2020). *How Learning Happens: Seminal Works in Educational Psychology and What They Mean in Practice*. Abingdon: Routledge.

Kistner, S., Rakoczy, K., Otto, B., Dignath-van Ewijk, C., Büttner, G. and Klieme, E. (2010). 'Promotion of Self-Regulated Learning in Classrooms: Investigating Frequency, Quality, and Consequences for Student Performance', *Metacognition and Learning*, 5 (2), pp. 157–171.

Kramarski, B., Mevarech, Z. R. and Arami, M. (2002). 'The Effects of Metacognitive Instruction on Solving Mathematical Authentic Tasks', *Educational Studies in Mathematics*, 49, pp. 225–250.

Kuhn, D. (1989). 'Children and Adults as Intuitive Scientists', *Psychological Review*, 96 (4), pp. 674–689.

Lemov, D. (2015). *Teach Like a Champion 2.0: 62 Techniques that Put Students on the Path to College*. San Francisco: Jossey-Bass.

Lemov, D., Woolway, E. and Yezzi, K. (2012). *Practice Perfect: 42 Rules for Getting Better at Getting Better*. San Francisco: Jossey-Bass.

Lindner, R. and Harris, B. (1992). 'The Development and Evaluation of a Self-Regulated Learning Inventory and Its Implications for Instructor-Independent Instruction', Ed 348 010. IR 015 747.

Mattock, P. (2019). *Visible Maths*. Carmarthen: Crown House Publishing Limited.

Mevarech, Z. R. (1999). 'Effects of Metacognitive Training Embedded in Cooperative Settings on Mathematical Problem Solving', *The Journal of Educational Research*, 92 (4). pp. 195–205.

Mevarech, Z. and Amrany, C. (2008). 'Immediate and Delayed Effects of Meta-Cognitive Instruction on Regulation of Cognition and Mathematics Achievement', *Metacognition Learning*, 3, pp. 147–157.

Mevarech, Z. R. and Kramarski, B. (1997). 'IMPROVE: A Multidimensional Method for Teaching Mathematics in Heterogeneous Classrooms', *American Research Journal*, 34 (2), pp. 365–394.

Morrison, R. M. (2015). 'The Question Matrix', Teacher Toolkit, available at: www. teachertoolkit.co.uk/2015/03/28/the-question-matrix/ (accessed 18 April 2022).

OFSTED (2015). 'National Priorities for the Teaching of Mathematics: A View from OFSTED', available at: https://slideplayer.com/slide/11062018/ (accessed 25 July 2022).

OFSTED (2019). 'Education Inspection Framework – Overview of Research', OFSTED, pp. 1–55.

Onu, V. C., Eskay, M., Igbo, J. N., Obiyo, N. and Agbo, O. (2012). 'Effect of Training in Math Metacognitive Strategy on Fractional Achievement of Nigerian Schoolchildren', *US–China Education Review*, 3, pp. 316–325.

Pershan, M. (2021). *Teaching Math with Examples*. Woodbridge: John Catt.

Peklaj, C. and Pecjak, S. (2002). 'Differences in Student's Self-Regulated Learning According to Achievement and Sex', *Studia Pscychologica*, 44 (1), pp. 29–45.

Perkins, D. (1992). *Smart Schools: Better Thinking and Learning for Every Child*. New York: The Free Press.

Rami, R. and Govil, P. (2013). 'Metacognition and Its Correlates', *International Journal of Advancement in Education and Social Sciences*, 1 (1), pp. 20–25.

Schraw, G. (1998). 'Promoting General Metacognitive Awareness', *Instructional Science*, 26, 113–125.

Sherrington, T. (2020). *Rosenshines Principles in Action*. Woodbridge: John Catt.

Sherrington, T. and Caviglioli, O. (2020). *Walkthrus*. Woodbridge: John Catt.

Sperling, R. A., Howard, B. C., Miller, L. A. and Murphy, C. (2002). 'Measures of Children's Knowledge and Regulation of Cognition', *Contemporary Educational Psychology*, 27, pp. 51–79.

Teong, S. K. (2003). 'The Effect of Metacognitive Training on Mathematical Word-Problem Solving', *Journal of Computer Assisted Learning*, 19 (1), pp. 46–55.

Toth, E. E., Klahr, D. and Chen, Z. (2000). 'Bridging Research and Practice: A Cognitively Based Classroom Intervention for Teaching Experimentation Skills to Elementary School Children', Carnegie Mellon University Research Showcase, Paper 337.

Topca, M. S. and Yilmaz-Tuzun, O. (2009). 'Elementary Students' Metacognition and Epistemological Beliefs Considering Science Achievement, Gender and Socioeconomic Status', *Elementary Education Online*, 8 (3), pp. 676–693.

Webb, J. (2021). *The Metacognition Handbook: A Practical Guide for Teachers and School Leaders*. Woodbridge: John Catt.

Willingham, D. T. (2011). 'Can Teachers Increase Students' Self-Control?', *American Educator*, Summer, pp. 22–27.

Zimmerman, B. J. (2002). 'Becoming a Self-Regulated Learner: An Overview', *Theory into Practice*, 41 (2), pp. 64–70.

Zohar, A. and Ben-David, A. (2008). 'Explicit Teaching of Meta-Strategic Knowledge in Authentic Classroom Situations', *Metacognition Learning*, 3, pp. 59–82.

Index